Supon Design Editions

ISBN 0-942604-47-4

Library of Congress Catalog Card Number 96-70276

Distributed to the trade in the United States and
Canada by:
Van Nostrand Reinhold
115 Fifth Avenue
New York, NY 10003

Distributed throughout the rest of the world by:
Hearst Books International
1350 Avenue of the Americas
New York, NY 10019

Published by:
Design Editions
1700 K Street, NW, Suite 400
Washington, DC 20006

Printed in Hong Kong

INTERNATIONAL

LOGOS AND

TRADEMARKS 3

Supon Design Group

ACKNOWLEDGMENTS

Project Director & Creative Director:
Supon Phornirunlit

Jacket Designer:
Andrew Dolan

Book Designer:
Richard Law

Hand Icon Illustrator:
Rodney Davidson

Editor:
Wayne Kurie

Associate Editor:
Greg Varner

Design Editors:
*Jacques Coughlin, Andrew Dolan, Maria Sese Paul,
Supon Phornirunlit, Sharisse Steber, Khoi Vinh*

Associate Book Designers:
*Brent Almond, Andrew Berman, Kimery Davis,
Mimi Eanes, Pum Mek-aroonreung,
Deborah Savitt, Lee Shaffer,
Sharisse Steber, Khoi Vinh*

Camera Services:
*CompuPrint, Washington, D.C.;
Color Imaging Center, Washington, D.C.;
The Photo Link, Washington, D.C.*

Photographers:
Oi Veerasarn, Debbie Accame

Corporate Identities
Designed by
Supon Design Group

A logo is like a streak of lightning, creating a sudden flash of recognition for a product or company. But before a logo can strike lightning in the public imagination, it must first streak through the mind of the designer. In a flash of inspiration—coming, as always, after considerable brainstorming thunder—the designer suddenly sees the solution to the problem.

And it's a big problem. The logo has a seemingly impossible task: it must immediately conjure up in the mind of the viewer the specific identity it's representing, and at the same time suggest the qualities of the business or product in question. Logos make the intangible visible. This is the reverse of the standard magician's trick of making an object invisible, but no less a wonder or charm. And on top of it all, the logo has to look good.

The importance of the logo can't be overstated. It must immediately suggest the type of goods or services being represented, even before the logo becomes recognizably fixed in the public mind. An attractive, eye-catching logo translates into sales, while a forgettable logo is passed by—and all of this happens quickly, often subconsciously. Sometimes a mark even takes on a life of its own, on t-shirts and in other applications differing from those for which it was originally created.

Studies have shown that trade figures—characters like Buster Brown—enter a child's consciousness even before the alphabet. This suggests the degree to which logos and trademarks have saturated our daily lives. How high the quality of a mark must be if it is to rise above the glut and distinguish itself with the public!

The marks in this book distinguish themselves in many ways. They came from nearly thirty countries all over the world—from Brazil, Czechoslovakia, China, Spain, Slovenia, Indonesia, and Iran. Of course, the majority of entries came from the United States. Thirty-eight states plus the District of Columbia are represented. Over 3,000 entries were submitted, of which fewer than 10 percent are included here. Our panel of judges spent more than two days sorting over the entries, gradually narrowing their choices to the work reproduced in this book. There was wide variety among the entries, of course: symbols and type; abstract and representational; updates on time-tested favorites and futuristic, high-tech marks were all submitted, in a variety of applications and styles.

The work you see in this book is out of context, isolated from its normal environment. As you look at these marks, imagine each one in its full application. Imagine sitting at your desk, opening correspondence written on one of the letterheads shown in this book, or pushing a grocery cart down a supermarket aisle and seeing these logos and packages. Think of seeing these signs on a street, or in a directory. That's where these images work their magic, communicating instantly to the world at large, often transcending language and culture. Corporations and financial institutions; food, drug, and beverage companies; service agencies and professional individuals of all kinds are placing greater emphasis on their marks than ever before.

Lightning seldom strikes in the same place twice. You might say, then, that a good logo almost defies the laws of nature. It has to be reproducible in a variety of contexts, capable of giving viewers a shock of recognition again and again.

We hope readers will find this book a valuable tool for enlarging their visual repertoire. We would like nothing better than to stimulate people to a heightened appreciation for this designer's art form, and to inspire them to create work of their own. Readers are invited to return the enclosed postcard with their comments. Any suggestions about how we might develop a successful International Logos & Trademarks IV would be appreciated.

In these pages, there are familiar images treated in fresh ways and a lot that is new and surprising. There are whimsical, playful designs, and an equal number of serious or dignified solutions. Whatever their style, these marks all share a common elegance and intelligence. I salute these creative artists and their good work, shown in the pages that follow. In addition, I would like to thank all those designers who participated for making this one of our most successful international logo and trademark competitions ever.

Supon Phornirunlit

Supon Phornirunlit is owner of Supon Design Group, Inc., where he serves as creative director and art director. Since founding the company in 1988, he and his design team have earned almost 700 awards, including recognition from every major national design competition. His work and studio profile have appeared in Graphis, Communication Arts, Print, Step by Step, and How. Supon has been recognized internationally in such publications as Page Magazine (Germany), Media Delite (Thailand), and Asia, Inc. (Hong Kong). Supon has served on the board of directors of the Art Directors' Club of Metropolitan Washington and is currently on the board of the Broadcast Designers' Association. Among the many awards he has received for his work are Gold Awards from both the Broadcast Designers Association and the AIGA's Baltimore Chapter. He regularly speaks and judges at various organizations and schools.

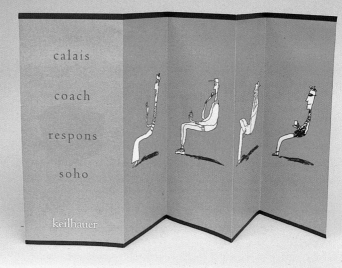

Corporate Identities
Designed by
Concrete Design Communications Inc.

I f you dive below the blue hues of conventional wisdom, you'll discover a disturbing truth about graphic designers and their contributions to the beautification of human life: creating visual symbols, corporate identifiers, and design systems sometimes has little to do with enlightened aesthetics or sanity. It's often about lunatic whim. That may sound cynical. It isn't. It's the reality we've all come to know and love about the design world.

Some time ago, a client asked us to create a logo for an important corporate document that was supposed to be emblematic of a global high-tech industry on the cutting edge of everything and anything. We responded with designs based on all sorts of computer, digital, and global imagery. The results were received with "ugh" and a mutter to "try again." The final design was a word set in futura extra bold oblique in the usual corporate blue hue. A colleague commented that he'd seen something similar on the side of a hockey equipment bag (please excuse the cultural bias, but Canadians resort to hockey-based analogy). Needless to say, you won't see that logo on the pages of this journal, although, if it did appear here, I'd defend it as a sublime work of unparalleled simplicity that resonates very deeply with the global aspirations of our client. So much for critical integrity.

What's the point of the story? I'm not sure. It doesn't say a lot about our ability to sell the right design for the right situation. But you can't win all the battles. More to the point: it raises questions about the state of a corporate design culture brought kicking and screaming into the modern era by Paul Rand, Saul Bass, and their peers. Really, how much have we evolved over the decades since design, as a corporate propaganda specialty, began to attract the attention of bauhaus-obsessed industrialists The short answer is: look at the skyscrapers, advertising campaigns, and billboards of the world. It's a landscape cluttered with circles, squares, and three-letter acronyms.

Meanwhile, listen to what design professionals have to say. You hear a lot of big words like "strategic," "global," and "image equity." One could argue that the profession has become comically oversophisticated. A colleague recently suggested that if you repeat the word "global" many times in succession, like a mantra, you sound like a turkey. Try it yourself. Global global global global. A turkey sound, right? Are we turkeys?

I say this not to be mean-spirited, but, somehow, the term "artist" has become a dirty word to graphic designers, mostly because we're trying to legitimize ourselves to those buying our services. We've become analytical and skilled at the art of proposal generation. We pitch business. We're problem-solvers. What are we, for God's sake, accountants? Business strategists?

And yet, despite our so-called transformation into "business strategists," there are many designers, and you'll see their work on these pages, who believe an essential part of what they do is intuitive and emotional. We design because of a need to express ourselves with pencils, pigments, paper, and pixels. We have an irrational but entirely human need to communicate. All the focus groups in the world won't change that.

My own philosophy—and that's a strong word—is that great design is likely to be achieved by the autocrat versus the "team player." European urban architecture is proof of that. I mean autocratic in the sense that design is an expression of very peculiar talents and skills that suffocate in strategy sessions and committee creative briefings. This doesn't mean great design can't result from collaboration. The architecture of older American towns is proof of that; enlightened people improvising together, like a jazz combo, abiding by commonly held standards and values in creating livable communities.

So there you have it. Hockey bag logos for high-tech companies. Designers crying the blues in the usual hues. And basketball teams using designers to search for the perfectly carnivorous dinosaur icon. But sports logos are another matter. The latest ones all appear to be manufactured at Sports Logo Central, where the palette seems limited to what looks good on the team mascot.

Do ten-year-old children really want to wear a duck on their chests?

I hope not.

Diti Katona

Soon after graduating with a BFA from Toronto's York University in 1984, Diti Katona and her husband, designer John Pylypczak, formed Concrete Design Communications Inc., based in Toronto. The bulk of Concrete's projects are high-profile corporate design work, though they also take on smaller projects. Diti's work has received international recognition in publications such as Communication Arts, Graphis, Print, How, and Lineagrafica. For entertainment, she makes occasional trips to Europe—notably Hungary, from whence her parents emigrated to Canada in 1956—but she admits she's a workaholic. "I never worry about whether we're as good as people say we are," she says. "We're only as good as our last job. The rest is all hype." Diti and John are the proud parents of two daughters, Camille and Greta.

Corporate Identities
Designed by
Hornall Anderson Design Works

COMMENTARY BY JACK ANDERSON

What's the secret, the magic behind a great logo design? Consider the weight the logo carries in an overall image program. Its longevity. Its need to survive and, even more importantly, to excel—in an unsheathed, black and white state with nothing to hide behind. As the cornerstone of a company or product marketing and graphics program, the logo establishes security and stability while allowing latitude for use in various applications. It's the distillation of all major company philosophies and attributes into a single mark. With these basic and critical criteria in mind, developing a successful logo is the most challenging of all design projects.

First and foremost, a great logo must solve the image challenge with good, solid communication. Once a simple, straightforward interpretation is created, a good logo will then deliver an added dimension, continuing to present messages a second and third time with layers of personality. This depth adds spirit and emotion to the mark and gives it an edge.

A successful logo cannot be created in a box. It is our obligation as designers to consider its usage and application. We must consider the category of business and the ultimate role the logo will play for the company. In a retail setting the logo is the anchor, most often taking a subordinate position to other components when applied to packaging, bags, and promotional materials. For a service organization or product the logo is that service or product. It is what people can visually identify with and remember. It is featured as the hero and is most always presented in the same fashion.

The logo is a core component to the overall image projected, but it works in tandem with other supporting elements. These elements help to provide elasticity for tone and manner of the image. As conditions, audiences, and messages change, this graphic is much more adaptable to keeping the look fresh and exciting. These changing elements, when melded with the logo, allow the whole image to adapt and grow while maintaining continuity and avoiding a static and dated presentation.

Today, a logo must excel in a host of mediums and applications, with more considerations to come as technologies continue to evolve. There are digital, on-line, print, fax, and low-grade reproduction requirements. Most recently, an added criterion is to create a logo than is "animateable." A mark that can come alive for multimedia and continue to allow for growth and extension in manipulable and constantly transforming mediums.

In the past, identity programs in general were expected to last anywhere between 10 and 20 years. With rapidly changing economies and markets and companies continually "morphing" (acquisitions, mergers, new technologies), in many cases logos are no longer expected to have an expansive life. This is an extremely freeing concept but one which we must not take lightly. On the good side, it results in more spontaneous and immediate solutions that are signs of the times. On the bad side, it leads to trendy, overly-illustrated presentations. Although in reality the life expectancy of the mark may not be timeless, the very basic characteristics of logos that are appealing and exciting are also those components that are intrinsic to human nature and transcend time, regional and philosophic boundaries.

I think as designers we are currently part of a strong movement. A design era that balances between the ultra simple, one-dimensional corporate logos of the 60s and 70s; the detailed, heavily illustrated solutions of the 80s; and the impersonal, carbon-copy response to the high-tech market. The heavy retro reference is subsiding. The smorgasbord approach with a multitude of type chaos and busyness are gone. The high-tech cliched treatments with a single line connecting points or many detailed lines are disappearing. The 90s seem to mean simple, clean logo designs—distilled to the essence without presenting plain or sterile impressions and adding a point of mystery or depth that is unique to the client.

Overall, a great logo design does what it has always done: communicates, solves the problem, adds dimension, survives time and different mediums. Our peripheral challenges evolve, but our basic assignment—to create clear, creative, and unique communication in an instant and beyond— remains constant.

Jack Anderson

Jack Anderson is one of the founding partners and guiding spirits of Hornall Anderson Design Works. He relishes the challenges of the business and plays an extremely active role in the design solutions the firm creates. His background includes experience in virtually all areas of design: development of corporate, brand, and product identity; collateral material; packaging and environmental graphics. His roster of clients is equally diverse, including Starbucks Coffee Company and Microsoft Corporation. He frequently judges design competitions, and his work has been repeatedly recognized by Communication Arts, the New York Art Directors Club, the American Institute of Graphic Arts, and Print Magazine, among many others. An avid cyclist and ski enthusiast, Jack lives in Seattle with his wife, Barb, and their daughter, Jessie.

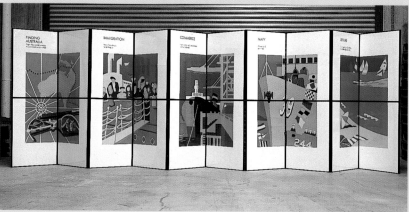

Corporate Identities
Designed by
Eymont Kin Yee Hulett

The logo or trademark is without doubt the ultimate "branding" tool. Far from being simply the latest buzz-word from the marketing gurus, branding (from the Old Norse brandr, meaning to burn) has been around since people first progressed from marking livestock to marking clay pots with a thumbprint or etched symbol to indicate a product's source and differentiate it from its competitors.

From these humble beginnings, the use of branding has been expanded in the twentieth century to include services and abstract concepts as well as tangible products, and along the way the target audience has developed a more sophisticated level of awareness and perception. Purpose, function, and concept are far more evident in modern trademarks than in those of earlier generations, when a simple typographic solution or a basic geometric symbol were enough to differentiate one business or product from another.

The most significant recent development in the logo's evolution within the corporate world is the fact that a company mark—the visual embodiment of a brand—is now seen as something of capital worth. A logo which is perceived as a guarantee of authenticity and quality can enhance sales and increase profit, giving it a very real monetary value on a corporation's balance sheets and making it a tradeable asset in itself.

So, at the same time as the designer's task is becoming more challenging, it is also becoming more clearly recognized by the client as playing a vitally important role in successful corporate strategy. This change in attitude on the part of business leaders is a welcome and somewhat overdue acknowledgement of the value of good design.

Another marked shift in emphasis which we as designers have had to adapt to in recent years is the rapid growth of new technologies—both products and services—which defy symbolism in concrete terms. Their intangible nature isn't subject to the distillation processes we tend to employ to get to the pure essence of the client's business, and a completely new approach to the task is now necessary. Especially in the field of computer technologies, progress continues to be so rapid and unpredictable that cutting-edge one year is superseded the next,

making the "timelessness" required of a good logo even more difficult to achieve.

The research period which precedes the creative process is becoming more crucial, as is the time involved in worldwide legal searches after the design has been approved, in cases where the client has plans for global distribution.

All this sounds as if the creative aspect of our work is being sacrificed to the demands of business, but in fact there is a growing awareness of the need for business to present a more human face, to take on more social and environmental responsibility. Consequently, the cold, hard-edged geometric symbols of the past are giving way to the lyrical, free-form, more organic symbols of the nineties. This current trend presents a different sort of challenge to the designer, but one which many of us welcome as an opportunity for freer expression of creativity.

In the quest for innovation and uniqueness of style in meeting the needs and expectations of clients, it's inevitable that our work will continue to evolve. Likewise, it's inevitable that the demands made on designers by the business world will also change.

It's impossible to predict the changes that will take place in logo and trademark design over the coming years, but the biggest challenge and the most fun lies in pushing our work in a completely new and original direction. Publications such as International Logos and Trademarks III provide an invaluable showcase for designers around the world who are doing just that.

Alison Hulett

Alison Hulett was born and raised in Scotland, educated in New Zealand, and lived and worked in the United States before moving to Australia. She was therefore an ideal candidate to join the multicultural design office of Anna Eymont (born, raised, and educated in Poland) and Myriam Kin-Yee (Vietnamese/Chinese, raised in Vanuatu and educated in Australia). The design work which is produced in their Sydney studio reflects the unique cultural mix of the three partners and the designers they employ. "Australia is a young, vibrant country," she says, "only just realizing its own identity, shaking off its European, derivative attitudes. Australian design is evolving in much the same way, and it's very exciting to be part of this process." Alison has received Gold, Silver, and Bronze Medals in the National Print Awards and numerous other honors.

BEST OF
OF
CATEGORY

BEST LOGO OF A COMPANY
Client: Hexagraph Fly Rods Company / Design Firm: Swieter Design

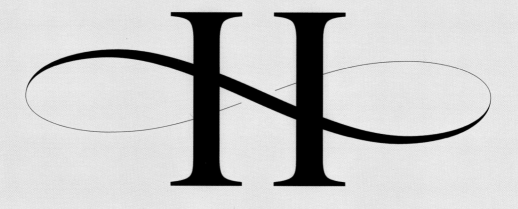

Client:
Hexagraph Fly Rods Company
Design Firm:
Swieter Design
United States
Dallas, Texas
Art Director:
John Swieter
Designer:
John Swieter

For fly-fishers, this beautiful and elegant mark for Hexagraph Fly Rods says it all, suggesting both the sport and the serenity it inspires. Judges praised its especially felicitous combination of typography and a representational icon.

John Swieter, the designer, is an avid fly-fisher himself. This work was commissioned in the middle of winter, causing him to suffer pangs of nostalgia, he says. "It was easy; I figured it out almost immediately, while driving. This rod is made of new materials, but is shaped like old-fashioned bamboo rods, so it feels traditional. We were trying to bridge two cultures—past and present—in the mark."

Client:
International Tennis Federation
Design Firm:
PPA Design Ltd.
Hong Kong
Art Director:
Byron Jacobs
Designer:
Byron Jacobs

For the International Tennis Federation's Annual General Meeting in Hong Kong, a true designer's feat was accomplished: the Chinese characters for "Hong Kong" and "Tennis" were shaped to represent this stylized tennis ball.

"Working with these Chinese characters was a bit difficult," designer Byron Jacobs says. "It's not my native language, but it's very appropriate for this job. After getting the words translated, I then had to contort the letter forms to give them a pleasing aesthetic balance. Though I'd worked with Chinese characters before, this was the first time I molded them."

BEST STATIONERY
Client: Pasifika Premier / Design Firm: Pasifika Premier

Client:
Pasifika Premier
Design Firm:
Pasifika Premier
Jakarta, Indonesia
Art Director:
Regina Rubino
Designers:
Robert Louey, Regina Rubino

Pasifika Premier, an international communications company head-quartered in Jakarta, Indonesia, designed this elegant stationery package for its own use. Our panel of judges praised its polish and its integration of polarities: white and black, night and day, east and west, sun and moon—all harmoniously combined to create a well thought-out look that is "rich, but not flashy or stuffy," as one of our judges remarked. "Everything is relevant," said another. "All the details tie in well with the basic concept."

Art director Regina Rubino remem-bers, "We covered all specs with the printer—even those details we considered the most minute. When the printed pieces arrived, every-thing seemed perfect—except there was no glue on the envelope flaps. We had to glue each envelope shut with a glue stick or staple it closed. As it happens, this is the standard here in Indonesia, and I did not think to request glue since every envelope that I had ever printed before came with glue on the flaps. Never assume anything."

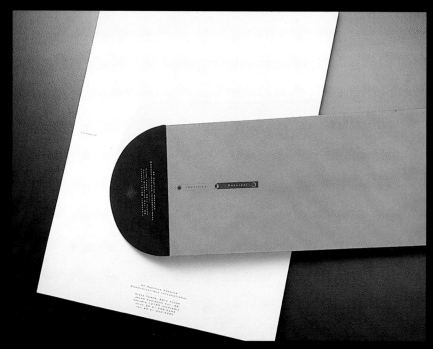

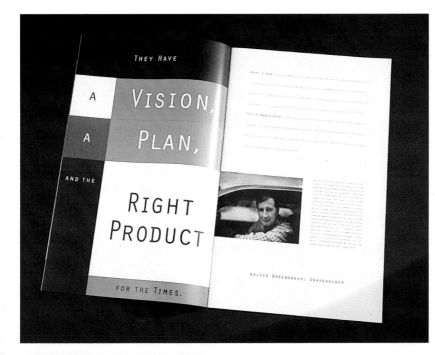

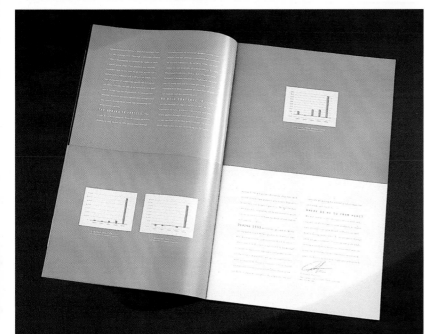

Client:
Signature Brands
Design Firm:
M. Vandenberg & Co.
Toronto, Ontario, Canada
Art Director:
Ron Vandenberg
Designers:
Ron Vandenberg, Jonathan Howells
Photographers:
Doug Forster, Vivian Gast

Signature Brands, a corn snack and specialty Mexican foods concern, impressed our judges with this unusual choice of format for its annual report. (One judge cheered the design firm's ability to convince the client to approve it.) The panel praised its attention-grabbing ability and fun look. "It's corporate, but not stodgy," said one. Another admired its "inviting and readable copy" and combinations of typography. All enjoyed its juxtaposition of pages or sections in color with those in black and white.

According to the designers, "The strategy was to position the company as a dynamic new player in the food-processing marketplace. The report's size made it easier to leave out on a table than to file away. Our idea was to reverse the focus of a traditional report by making the quotes the key visuals and using the photographs as support. We told the story of the company through the eyes of its shareholders."

BEST PACKAGING
Client: Foote, Cone & Belding for Adolph Coors Brewing Company / Design Firm: Primo Angeli Inc.

Client:
Foote, Cone & Belding for Adolph
Coors Brewing Company
Design Firm:
Primo Angeli Inc.
San Francisco, California
Art Directors:
(Primo Angeli, Inc.) Primo Angeli,
Carlo Pagoda; (Libby Perszyk
Kathman) Ray Perszyk, Howard
McIlvain; (Coors) Pam Moorehead;
(FCB) George Chadwick
Designers:
(PAI) Carlo Pagoda, Ed Cristman,
Vicki Cero; (LPK) Bob Johnson,
Jim Gabel, Mary Jo Betz, Bradd
Bush, Liz Grubow, Andy Scott,
Rowland Heming

Judges applauded the elegance and
simplicity of this package for Zima,
a clear malt beverage intended as
an alternative to beer and other
alcohol drinks. "There's a nice interplay between the molding of the
glass and the clear liquid inside,"
one judge observed. All considered
this an attractive bottle and agreed
that it was excellent packaging for a
clear product. They also thought
the design succeeded in suggesting
the clean, pure qualities touted by
the manufacturer.

"This was a case in which we were
designing the packaging before the
product was produced," according
to designer Primo Angeli. "One of
the key issues was that this was
neither a beer, nor a cooler, nor a
soda. It's a malt, a rather new category in the United States. The look
had to say, 'This is something different.' It had to have an exotic look
to it—as if it might be imported—
so we had to create a look that didn't
exist before."

Client:
Craig Singleton Hollomon Architec
Design Firm:
Communication Arts Company
Jackson, Mississippi
Art Director:
Hilda Stauss Owen
Designer:
Hilda Stauss Owen
Photographer:
Gretchen Halen

This unusual signage for Craig
Singleton Hollomon Architects
makes exceptionally pleasing use o
color and typography. "It's clever
and beautiful," as one judge sum-
marized it. Appropriately for an
architectural firm, this sign has a
very structural look.

Hilda Stauss Owen, who designed
the logo and then supervised its
application here, says, "This sign
was a lot of fun to do, because this
firm was willing to try something di
ferent. They like to experiment with
materials, so that's what we did.
Since steel is fundamental to architectural projects, the sign is con-
structed out of raw steel. Using var
ous abrasion techniques, we tooled
everything outside the logo's edge

JUDGES'
CHOICE
CATEGORY

JUDGES' CHOICE: LOGO
Client: Bow Wow Barber / Design Firm: Sibley/Peteet Design, Inc.

Client:
Bow Wow Barber
Design Firm:
Sibley/Peteet Design, Inc.
Austin, Texas
Art Director:
Derek Welch
Designer:
Derek Welch

The humor of this crossover idea
for Bow Wow Barber dog groomers
pleased our judges. "This shows
wit and whimsy," one said.

Client:
Cybersport Ltd.
Design Firm:
Siren
Vancouver, British Columbia,
Canada
Art Director:
Jim Yue
Designer:
Jim Yue

A strong sense of motion comes
through in this logo for CyberSport,
a distributor of cycling products.
The simplicity of this logo works
exceedingly well with the letter
form.

JUDGES' CHOICE: LOGO

Client: Dallas Symphony Orchestra / Design Firm: RBMM/The Richards Group

Client:
Dallas Symphony Orchestra
Design Firm:
RBMM/The Richards Group
Dallas, Texas
Art Director:
Horacio Cobos
Designer:
Horacio Cobos
Illustrator:
Horacio Cobos

The appropriateness of this classically drawn logo for the Dallas Symphony Orchestra impressed our judges. "It looks like the bass clef," one judge pointed out, "and also brings to mind music resonating from a source. It almost looks like an amphitheater." All of these possibilities are integrated nicely into a very pretty symbol.

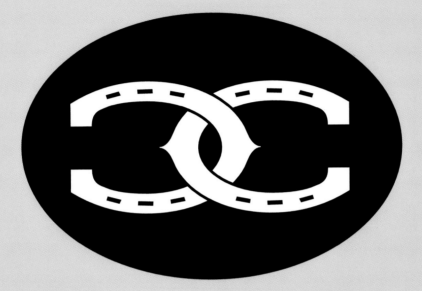

Client:
Dixie Chicks
Design Firm:
Sibley/Peteet Design, Inc.
Austin, Texas
Art Director:
Rex Peteet
Designer:
Rex Peteet
Illustrator:
Rex Peteet

The stylized incorporation of letters
in this logo for the Dixie Chicks, an
all-cowgirl country music band,
pleased our judges.

JUDGES' CHOICE: LOGO
Client: Ellis Electric / Design Firm: Toma and Associates

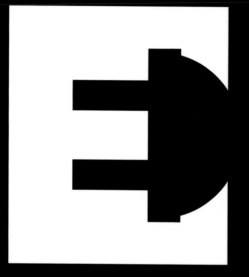

Client:
Ellis Electric
Design Firm:
Toma and Associates
Denver, Colorado
Art Director:
Sara Ohlson
Designer:
Sara Ohlson

The smooth interplay between
typography and a representational
icon in this electrician's trademark
create an effect similar to that of an
optical illusion, pulling your eye
back and forth between the letter
'E' and the plug.

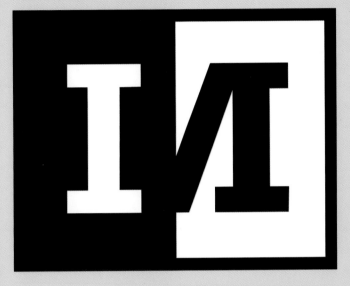

Client:
HGH Publishing Ltd.
Design Firm:
Telmet Design Associates
Toronto, Ontario, Canada
Art Director:
Tiit Telmet
Designers:
Robert Farrell, Joseph Gault

This clever mark for *InfoMedia Magazine* plays nicely with positive and negative spaces. Judges praised its *trompe l'oeil* effect: "There's no 'M', but you definitely see one," a judge remarked.

Client:
Ideas & Solutions
Design Firm:
Lambert Design Studio
Dallas, Texas
Art Director:
Christie Lambert
Designer:
Joy Cathey Price

Ideas and Solutions, an auditing
and consulting firm, helps corporations find ways to save on utility
bills. It is aptly represented by this
solution, in which the placement of
type entering and exiting the maze
won special admiration.

Client:
Jabolko
Design Firm:
KROG
Ljubljana, Slovenia
Art Director:
Edi Berk
Designer:
Edi Berk

In this elegantly proportioned logo, the computer tape at the core of the apple (in English, the name of this computer typesetting business, Jabolko, is translated as "apple") is quickly identified.

JUDGES' CHOICE: LOGO
Client: Quebecor Integrated Media / Design Firm: Hornall Anderson Design Works, Inc.

QUEBECOR INTEGRATED MEDIA

Client:
Quebecor Integrated Media
Design Firm:
Hornall Anderson
Design Works, Inc.
Seattle, Washington
Art Director:
Jack Anderson
Designers:
Jack Anderson, Heidi Favour,
Mary Chin Hutchison, Mary Hermes

An offset printer with a full range of
services, Quebecor chose a high-
tech look with this subtle mark.

R

りんてつ

Client:
Rintetsu
Design Firm:
The Design Associates Company, Ltd.
Tokyo, Japan
Art Directors:
The Design Associates

Rintetsu is a coastal Japanese railway specializing in the transport of industrial materials. Its logo conveys the speed of the train and also keeps the firm's name in mind: the Japanese characters under the 'R' spell it out.

JUDGES' CHOICE: LOGO
Client: Rod Ralston Photography / Design Firm: Hornall Anderson Design Works, Inc.

Client:
Rod Ralston Photography
Design Firm:
Hornall Anderson
Design Works, Inc.
Seattle, Washington
Art Director:
Jack Anderson
Designers:
Jack Anderson, Julie Keenan,
Mary Chin Hutchison

Conceptually, this logo for Rod
Ralston, a Seattle photographer, is
very strong. "Photography comes
immediately to mind," said one of
our judges. Another admired its
classic type, saying, "This logo will
never go out of date."

JUDGES' CHOICE: LOGO

Client: Sibley/Peteet Design, Inc. / Design Firm: Sibley/Peteet Design, Inc.

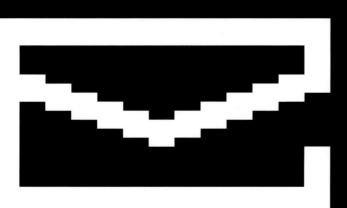

Client:
Sibley/Peteet Design, Inc.
Design Firm:
Sibley/Peteet Design, Inc.
Dallas, Texas
Art Director:
Tom Kirsch
Designer:
Tom Kirsch

Judges admired the way this icon,
developed for internal use on out-
going electronic mail, began with
the representation of an envelope
which was then made into an 'e'.

JUDGES' CHOICE: LOGO

Client: Slovenian Railway / Design Firm: KROG

Client:
Slovenian Railway
Design Firm:
KROG
Ljubljana, Slovenia
Art Director:
Edi Berk
Designer:
Edi Berk

In this streamlined mark, we see both the railroad and a subtle reference to the 'S' of Slovenian Railway.

Client: Watchworks / Design Firm: Byron Jacobs

Client:
Watchworks
Design Firm:
Byron Jacobs
Hong Kong
Art Director:
Byron Jacobs
Designer:
Byron Jacobs

With its clever stylization of the letter 'W' worked into a watch's face,
this logo for Watchworks, a clock
and watch manufacturer in Hong
Kong, was chosen for a variety of
applications.

JUDGES' CHOICE: LOGO
Client: Wild Hog Records / Design Firm: Walker Creative, Inc.

Client:
Wild Hog Records
Design Firm:
Walker Creative, Inc.
Fayetteville, Arkansas
Art Director:
Tim Walker
Designer:
Tim Walker

The playful combination of two
graphics for Wild Hog, an independent record label, produced this
inspired solution.

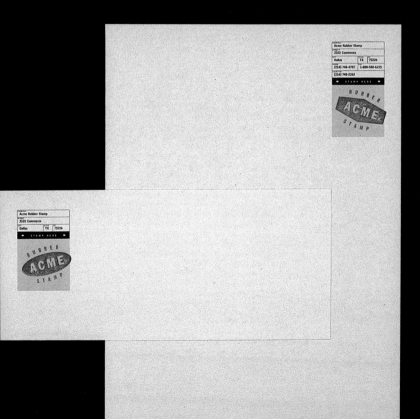

Client:
ACME Rubber Stamp Company
Design Firm:
Peterson & Company
Dallas, Texas
Art Director:
Dave Eliason
Designer:
Dave Eliason

This solution for Acme Rubber Stamp pleased the judges with its fresh look. "I like this because it takes what could have been a cliché and rejuvenates it," said one.

Client:
Cynthia Rudge
Design Firm:
Concrete Design
Communications Inc.
Toronto, Ontario, Canada
Art Directors:
John Pylypczak, Diti Katona
Designer:
Susan McIntee
Illustrator:
Mike Constable

A marketing consultant, Cynthia Rudge's only criteria is that work must be fun. Her business philosophy is reflected in this attractive design, which aptly breaks the rules by combining business-like and playful elements to form an unexpected solution.

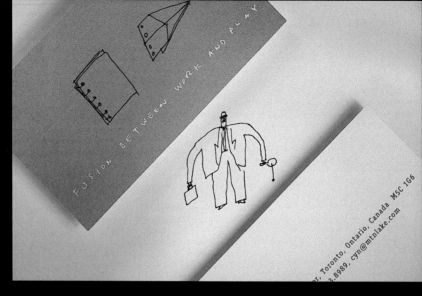

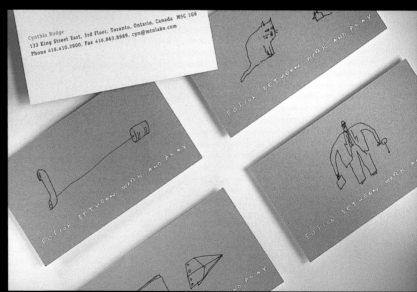

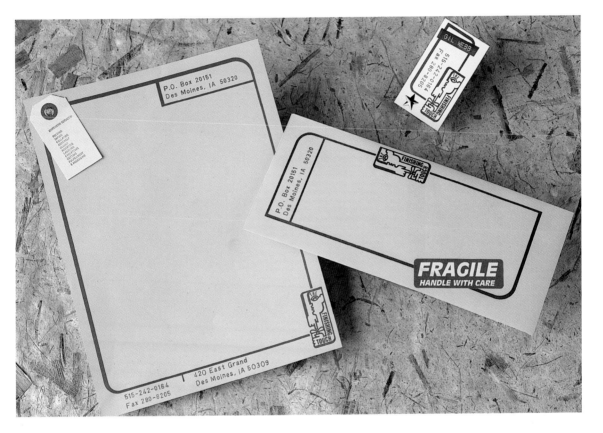

Client:
The Finishing Touch
Design Firm:
Sayles Graphic Design
Des Moines, Iowa
Art Director:
John Sayles
Designer:
John Sayles
Illustrator:
John Sayles

Judges praised the strong concept of this stationery solution for The Finishing Touch, a Des Moines, Iowa, bindery. The company is fittingly represented by this hands-on kit, in which the business card alone features label tape, a stick-on star, and a rubber stamp.

JUDGES' CHOICE: STATIONERY
Client: Tarzan Communications Inc. / Design Firm: Tarzan Communications Inc.

Client:
Tarzan Communications Inc.
Design Firm:
Tarzan Communications Inc.
Montreal, Quebec, Canada
Art Directors:
Daniel Fortin, George Fok,
Steve Spazuk
Designers:
George Fok, Daniel Fortin

The originality of this stationery for
Tarzan Communications, a Montreal
design studio, won the admiration
of our judges, who also cited the
subdued color and typography as
winning elements. "It's very clean,"
said one judge, "and the wave of
the paper is a subtle reference to
printed materials," since paper is
often represented symbolically by
a wave.

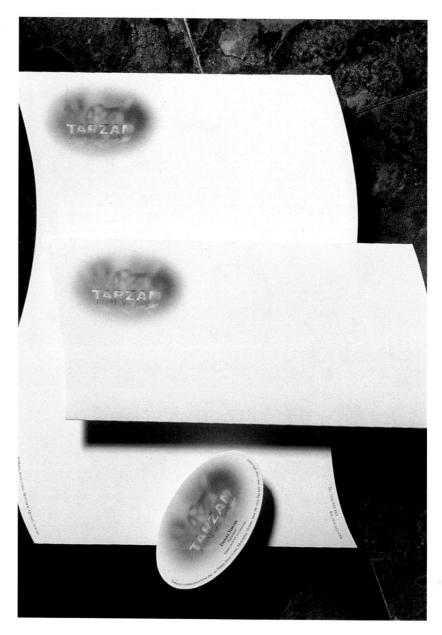

Client:
Major & Tom
Design Firm:
MaD House Design
Sydney, New South Wales, Australia
Art Director:
Donna Cavanough
Designer:
Michelle Pullen
Photographer:
Willem Rethmeier

Major & Tom, an Australian furniture-restoration company specializing in timbers unique to Australia, chose this elegant package showing a naturally formed wood shaving to suggest style and workmanship. Judges praised its use of unexpected colors and classic type.

Client:
Starbucks Coffee Company
Design Firm:
Hornall Anderson
Design Works, Inc.
Seattle, Washington
Art Director:
Jack Anderson
Designers:
Jack Anderson, Julie Lock,
Mary Chin Hutchison
Illustrator:
Linda Frichtel
Photograher:
Michael Baciu

This report for Starbucks, the fast-growing coffeehouse chain, combines an earthy look with sophisticated polish. Judges praised the choice of natural, unbleached paper, good use of the short sheet, and graceful blend of photography with illustration and icons. Graphs presented in an untraditional way relate well to the whole design.

Client:
Applied Control Systems
Design Firm:
Y's Communication
St. Leonard's, New South Wales,
Australia
Creative Director:
Phil Young

Applied Control Systems, an engineering company, chose an interesting fold-out format and an unusual color combination for this attractive brochure. It makes good use of typography and gives readers "a technological feel without sensory overload," in the words of one judge.

JUDGES' CHOICE: ANNUAL REPORT
Client: Lasertechnics, Inc. / Design Firm: Vaughn Wedeen Creative

Client:
Lasertechnics, Inc.
Design Firm:
Vaughn Wedeen Creative
Albuquerque, New Mexico
Art Director:
Steve Wedeen
Designer:
Steve Wedeen
Photographer:
Michael Barley

This artfully done report for Lasertechnics, a laser-marking and photo-imaging firm, pleased judges with the way its design echoed the division of one company into two, one centered on package coding and the other on photo imaging. Duality became its organizing principle, as the report nicely combined textured paper with smooth, monotone with full color, and perforated top and bottom halves to reflect the split.

the perseverance and ingenuity is as enormous as it is deserved. They are why I can say with confidence that your past patience and future expectations as shareholders in Lasertechnics have never held more merit.

Sincerely,

Richard M. Clarke

Chairman and Chief Executive Officer,

Lasertechnics Inc.

AL6724990N6

nordwest finanz-vermögensberatung
Am Brill 1–3
28195 Bremen

AF2573668A7

Telefon 0421 179 22 83

A1367065A9

Client:
Nordwest Finanz,
Vermögensberatung
Design Firm:
Kleiner & Bold
Bremen, Germany
Designers:
Tammo F. Bruns, Frank Schulte,
Karsten Unterberger

The classic look of this brochure
Nordwest, a German financial ins
tution, is proof that a traditional
approach can still yield attractive
and interesting results. This
brochure suggests the solid char
teristic of the institution, and
inspires calm trust. All of its elements, from the photography to
choice of paper, combine to repre
sent reliability and elegance.

AU1016537N5

AK7864177U6

Von vornherein fest gegründet

Mit unserer Hilfe werden aus guten
Ideen Unternehmen. Partnerschaftlich
prüft die *nwf* Existenzgründungsvor-
haben. Ohne Wenn und Aber werden
alle Chancen und Risiken offengelegt.
Gewinnschwellenanalysen, detaillier-
te Finanzpläne und fundierte Gewinn-
und Verlustprognosen sorgen für
eine realistische Basis. Alle Kreditbe-
dingungen werden von der *nwf* er-
arbeitet, der Zins- und Tilgungsplan
u.v.m. Auch bei der Beantragung
öffentlicher Mittel sind wir behilflich.
Unsere Checkliste für Existenzgrün-
der läßt keine ökonomische Frage un-
beantwortet.

So baut die *nwf* Existenzgründern ein
tragfähiges Fundament. Die ersten
drei Jahre des neuen Unternehmens
werden zu einer kalkulierbaren
Größe, über deren Risiko das unter-
nehmerische Können entscheidet.
Solide Zahlen wiederum geben Selbst-
gewißheit und jenen Optimismus,
der Kunden mitreißt und das Geschäft
zum Blühen bringt.

Ausländische Währun-
gen aus Australien,
Japan, Israel, Malta und
Irland; Mit dem wach-
senden Vertrauen in
den Staat wuchs das
Vertrauen ins Papier-
geld. Jede Staatsbank
garantierte dem Ein-
reicher einer Banknote,
daß das Papier in die
entsprechende Menge
Goldes getauscht
würde. Glücklicherwei-
se haben dies die
Banknoteninhaber nie-
mals verlangt.

ent:
nergy, Inc.
sign Firm:
ford Selbert Design
laborative
nbridge, Massachusetts
Director:
in Perkins
signer:
Breidenbach

s "X-rated" brochure for
nergy bicycle wheels is appropri-
ly fast-paced, suggesting speed
motion. "It has good, attention-
ting copy and seems just right
its audience," said one of our
ges. "I like that it has funky
ography, but is still highly read-
e," said another. "Its use of
tallic ink is well suited to its sub-
t matter," said a third.

We want **YOU** to be (X)-rated **too**

"Spinergy are the fastest, most versatile wheels available." Marzeno Berglund, Team Bodywise

"Spinergy wheels are the best in the world." Giovanni Lombardi, Team Polti

IT'S AN OFFER YOU CAN'T REFUSE

You give your customers what they want: to test-ride the fastest wheels on the planet — the Spinergy rev-X.

You can purchase these test wheels at a great discount, and Spinergy will direct consumers in your area to your shop through our national advertising campaign.

You'll be X-rated. And thrilled with excited sales!

The Spinergy X-rated program includes:

- One pair of Spinergy rev-X test wheels at the discounted price of $450, and a second pair in the regular price.
- National advertising (in Velonews, Winning, Inside Triathlon, and Triathlete) with consumers in your area directed to your shop.
- Spinergy rev-X sales licensee.
- An X-rated wall poster (enclosed...see next page).
- And demo wheel stickers.

lighter, more aerodynamic

[call now!]

ornament   203 762-9198
if you're a **TREK** dealer   800 313-8735
if you're a ●●●● dealer   800 7-CODA-96

(all the dealers are

(doin' it)

Ride on 'em   *get hot*

see if you like it

see if it   **feels good**

then   # decide

we bet you will

faster **faster** faster   WANT MORE

"I wouldn't ride something that I didn't think was the fastest." Karen Smyers

the best you'll

ever ride

race wins

1st Place	3rd stage, Tour of Italy	Gianni Bugno (Polti)
1st Place	Tour of Yugoslavia	Eddie Grigus
2nd Place	U.S. Pro Championship	Bruno Boscardin (Polti)
2nd Place	U.S. Pro Championship	Brian Walton (Saturn)
2nd Place	Hawaii Ironman	Karen Smyers
1st Place	La Jolla Grand Prix	Jeanne Golay (Saturn)
Gold Medal	Goodwill Games	Brooke Blackwelder (Bodywise)
Silver Medal	Goodwill Games	Karen Ritter-Livingston (World Team)
Overall Winner	World Cup Cyclocross Series	Daniele Pontoni (Brescialat)
1st Place	Italian National Cyclocross Champ	Daniele Pontoni (Brescialat)
1st Place	U.S. National Cyclocross Champ	Jan Wiejak (US Mangoes/Scott)
3rd Place	World Cyclocross Champ	Richard Groenendaal
1st Place	U.S. National Cyclocross Champ	Jonathon Page
1st Place	Dutch National Cyclocross Champ	Adri Van der Poel (Collstrop)
1st Place	Noda de Sausage (TT)	Sergei Uchakov (Polti)
1st Place	Pan Am Games Triathlon	Karen Smyers
Gold Medal	Pan Am Games Triathlon	Karen Smyers
1st Place	Redlands Classic	Linda Brenneman (Cycle Velco)
1st Place	3 Days of the Dolfinne (TT)	Maurizio Fondriest (Lampre)
1st Place	Vasilis Criterium	Dave McCook (Montgomery/Bell)
1st Place	Amstel Gold - Holland	Mauro Gianetti (Polti)
1st Place	89'er Stage Race	Dawn Marie Buehl

e,
e,
do

ain, a
waters,
n their
ements.
ook, and
end felici-
uct's

Client:
The Great Atlantic & Pacific
Company of Canada
Design Firm:
M. Vandenberg & Co.
Toronto, Ontario, Canada
Art Director:
Ron Vandenberg
Designers:
Ron Vandenberg, Jonathan Howells
Illustrator:
Steven Chien
Photographer:
Pat Lacroix

Judges enjoyed these playful package designs for Master Choice frozen pizza, which they considered most appropriate given pizza's status as the preeminent fun, social food. From the pepperoni decorating the gangster's lapel to the peppers in the bandit's ammunition belt, they appreciated the whimsy of these illustrations. One judge especially enjoyed the variety of typography used in these informative and entertaining designs.

JUDGES' CHOICE: PACKAGING
Client: Kider's Shoes Store / Design Firm: Y Design

Client:
Kider's Shoes Store
Design Firm:
Y Design
Walnut, California
Art Director:
Clement Yip
Designer:
Clement Yip
Photographer:
Kirk Kiu

This bag from Kider's Shoe Store delighted our judges with its strong concept. They admired the handle's bright and witty reference, and agreed that the eye-catching colors and general playfulness demonstrate that Kider's is a fun place to shop for children's shoes.

Client:
Le Bar Bat
Design Firm:
Louey/Rubino Design Group
Santa Monica, California
Art Director:
Robert Louey
Designers:
Robert Louey, Lisa Tauber
Photographers:
Merlyn Rosenberg, Sidney Cooper

"Without actually showing the bats, this logo makes us feel their presence," one of our judges observed, commenting on the aptness of the Gothic typography used on objects such as a membership card and pin, for a private Hong Kong nightclub.

JUDGES' CHOICE: APPLICATION
Client: Jonkers Hofstee Film / Design Firm: Designers Company

Client:
Jonkers Hofstee Film
Design Firm:
Designers Company
Amsterdam, The Netherlands
Art Director:
Ron Van Der Vlugt
Designer:
Ron Van Der Vlugt

This playful stationery package for
a Dutch film company makes good
use of color and was a good fit for
the client, suggesting motion,
focus, and color—attributes it
shares with film.

Client:
Alki Bakery
Nature of Business:
Bakery and cafe
Design Firm:
Hornall Anderson
Design Works, Inc.
Art Director:
Jack Anderson
Designers:
Jack Anderson, David Bates
Illustrator:
David Bates

Client:
Allien
Nature of Business:
Stationery store
Design Firm:
Félix Beltrán + Asociados
Art Director:
Félix Beltrán
Designer:
Félix Beltrán

Client:
Alice Kordenbrock,
Alice's Handweaving
Nature of Business:
Weaver
Design Firm:
Kirby Stephens Design, Inc.
Art Director:
Bill Jones
Designer:
Bill Jones

Alice's Handweaving

Client:
Studio NOB
Design Firm:
Packaging Create Inc.
Art Director:
Akio Okumura
Designer:
Katsuji Minami

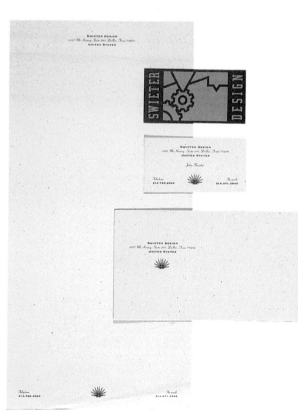

Client:
Swieter Design United States
Design Firm:
Swieter Design United States
Art Director:
John Swieter
Designer:
John Swieter

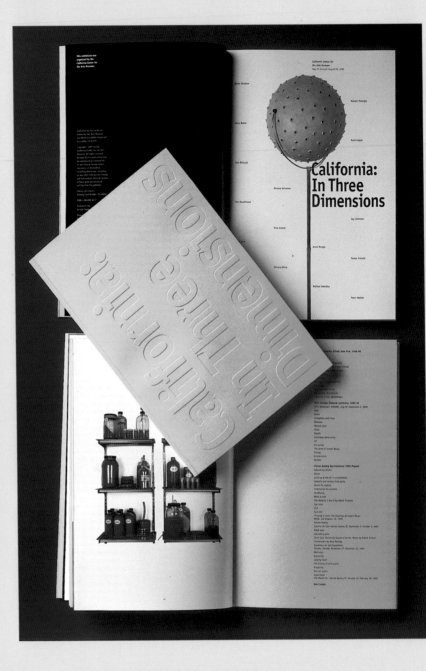

Client:
California Center for the Arts
Nature of Business:
Museum
Design Firm:
Mires Design, Inc.
Art Director:
John Ball
Designers:
John Ball, Deborah Fukoshima

Client:
Nike, Inc.
Nature of Business:
Sportswear manufacturer
Design Firm:
Pinkhaus
Art Director:
John Norman
Designer:
John Norman
Illustrator:
John Norman

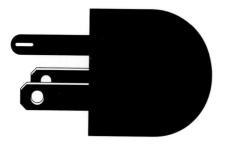

Client:
David Mathis, B.S.E.E.
Nature of Business:
Electrical engineer
Design Firm:
Varela Graphics
Art Director:
Raul Varela
Designer:
Raul Varela

Client:
Debrann Barr
Nature of Business:
Harpist
Designer:
Susan Mosdell

Client:
John Mancini,
Best Case Solutions, Inc.
Design Firm:
Michael Stanard, Inc.
Art Director:
Michael Stanard
Designers:
Marc C. Fuhrman,
Kristy Vandeherckhove

Client:
The Atlantic Group
Design Firm:
The Atlantic Group
Art Director:
Colleen Sion
Designer:
Colleen Sion

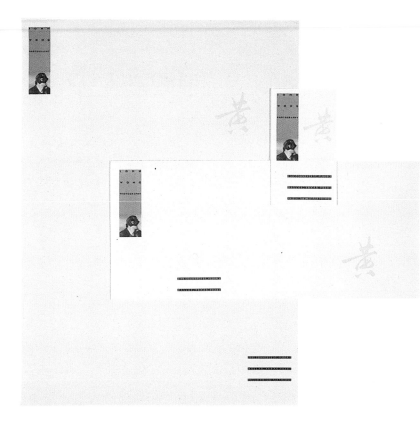

Client:
John Wong Photography
Nature of Business:
Photography studio
Design Firm:
Peterson & Company
Art Director:
Bryan L. Peterson
Designer:
Bryan L. Peterson

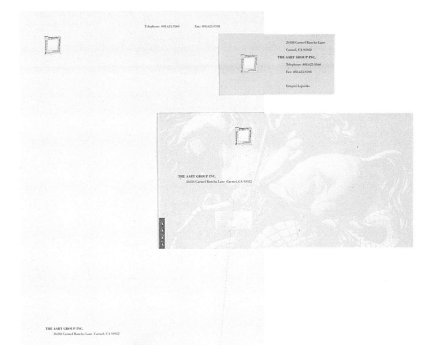

Client:
The AART Group
Nature of Business:
Art gallery
Design Firm:
Sackett Design Associates
Art Director:
Mark Sackett
Designer:
Mark Sackett
Illustrator:
Chris Yaryan

Client:
Stratus Computers
Design Firm:
Clifford Selbert Design
Collaborative
Art Director:
Lynn Riddle
Designers:
Iesa Figueroa, Jeff Breidenbach
Photographer:
Greg Wostrel

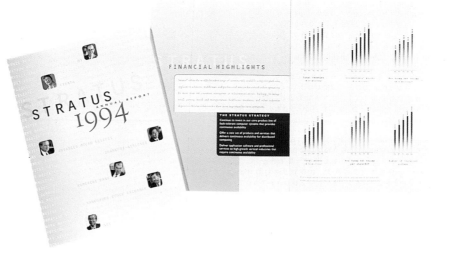

Client:
Avid Technology
Design Firm:
Clifford Selbert Design
Collaborative
Art Director:
Lynn Riddle
Designers:
Iesa Figueroa, Jeff Breidenbach
Photographer:
Greg Wostrel

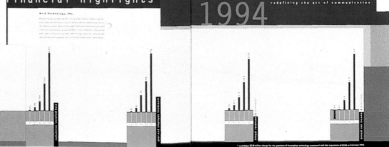

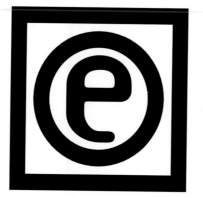

Client:
Fujitsu
Nature of Business:
Envoy, monthly technical journal
Design Firm:
Swieter Design United States
Art Director:
John Swieter
Designer:
Mark Ford

Client:
ElseWare Corporation
Nature of Business:
Software developer
Design Firm:
Hornall Anderson
Design Works, Inc.
Art Director:
Jack Anderson
Designers:
Jack Anderson, Debra Hampton,
Leo Raymundo

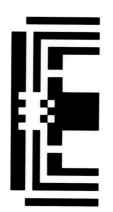

Client:
IPN-Electrónica
Nature of Business:
Electronics company
Design Firm:
Félix Beltrán + Asociados
Art Director:
Félix Beltrán
Designer:
Patricia Rojas

Client:
Virgin Interactive Entertainment
Nature of Business:
Entertainment company
Design Firm:
Margo Chase Design
Art Director:
Margo Chase
Designer:
Margo Chase
Illustrator:
Margo Chase
Photographer:
Sidney Cooper

Client:
Smith Sport Optics, Inc.
Nature of Business:
Sunglass manufacturer
Design Firm:
Hornall Anderson
Design Works, Inc.
Art Director:
Jack Anderson
Designers:
Jack Anderson, David Bates

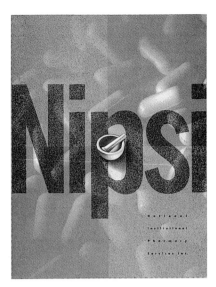

LEFT

Client:
NIPSI
Nature of Business:
Pharmacy services provider
Design Firm:
Vaughn Wedeen Creative
Art Director:
Rick Vaughn
Designer:
Dan Flynn
Photographer:
Michael Barley

RIGHT

Client:
Thermo Instruments
Nature of Business:
Environmental control instruments
manufacturer
Design Firm:
Clifford Selbert Design
Collaborative
Art Director:
Julia Daggett
Designers:
Darren Namaye, April Skinnard
Photographer:
Greg Wostrel

Client:
ColorAd Printers
Nature of Business:
Printer
Design Firm:
Jerry Takigawa Design
Art Director:
Jerry Takigawa
Designers:
Glenn Johnson, Jerry Takigawa
Illustrator:
Jay Galster (Photoshop)
Photographer:
Jerry Takigawa

Client:
Terri Gibbs Photography
Nature of Business:
Photographer
Design Firm:
Sibley/Peteet Design, Inc.
Art Director:
Derek Welch
Designer:
Derek Welch
Illustrator:
Derek Welch

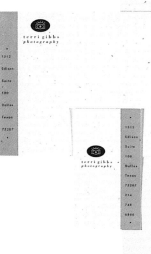

Client:
InfoFusion
Nature of Business:
Institutional research, writing,
and design firm
Design Firm:
Peterson & Company
Art Director:
Bryan L. Peterson
Designer:
Bryan L. Peterson

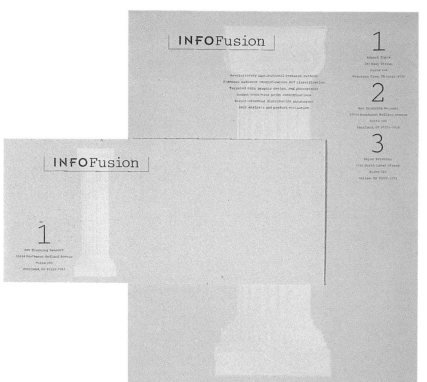

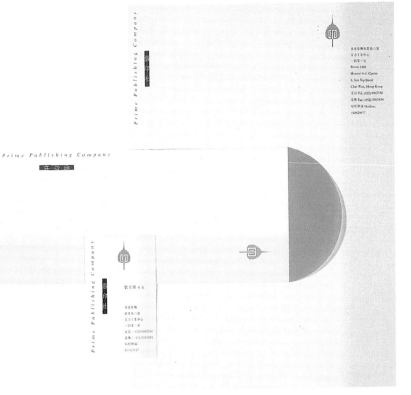

Client:
Prime Publishing Co.
Design Firm:
Kan Tai-keung Design
& Associates Ltd.
Art Director:
Freeman Lau Siu Hong
Designer:
Freeman Lau Siu Hong

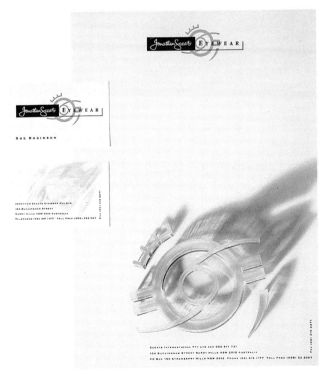

Client:
Jonathan Sceats Eyewear
Design Firm:
Harcus Design
Art Director:
Annette Harcus
Designer:
Stephanie Martin
Photographer:
Keith Arnold

Client:
Hotel Huasteca
Nature of Business:
Hotel
Design Firm:
Félix Beltrán + Asociados
Art Director:
Félix Beltrán
Designer:
Félix Beltrán

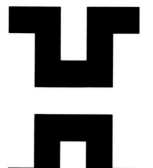

Client:
Type House
Nature of Business:
Typesetter
Design Firm:
Félix Beltrán + Asociados
Art Director:
Félix Beltrán
Designer:
Félix Beltrán

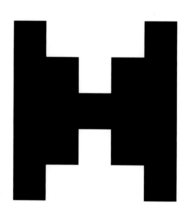

Client:
I. Hoffman & Associates
Nature of Business:
New media techniques consultant
Design Firm:
Concrete Design Communications
Inc., Toronto
Art Directors:
John Pylypczak, Diti Katona
Designer:
John Pylypczak

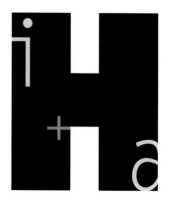

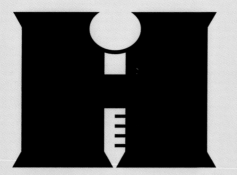

Client:
HomeWorks
Nature of Business:
Residential remodeling company
Design Firm:
Sibley/Peteet Design, Inc.
Art Director:
Rex Peteet
Designer:
Rex Peteet
Illustrator:
Rex Peteet

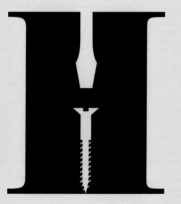

Client:
J. M. Hooker Construction
Nature of Business:
Residential construction company
Design Firm:
Walker Creative, Inc.
Art Director:
Tim Walker
Designer:
Tim Walker

Client:
Herbal Connection
Nature of Business:
Herb merchant
Design Firm:
Roman Duszek
Art Director:
Roman Duszek
Designer:
Roman Duszek

Client:
Deleo Clay Tile Company
Design Firm:
Mires Design, Inc.
Art Director:
José Serrano
Designer:
José Serrano
Illustrator:
Nancy Stahl

Client:
DogStar Design
Design Firm:
DogStar Design
Designer:
Rodney Davidson
Illustrator:
Rodney Davidson
Copywriter:
Rodney Davidson

Client:
Kwasha Lipton
Design Firm:
Toni Schowalter Design
Art Director:
Toni Schowalter
Designer:
Toni Schowalter
Photographer:
Bard Martin

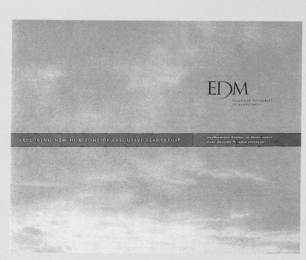

Client:
Weatherhead School of
Management
Design Firm:
Epstein, Gutzwiller, Schultz
& Partners
Art Directors:
Steve Schultz,
Victoria Quintos Robinson
Designers:
Steve Schultz,
Victoria Quintos Robinson

Client:
Graham Wright Interactive
Nature of Business:
Interactive multimedia communications firm
Design Firm:
Critt Graham & Associates
Art Director:
Gregg Snyder
Designer:
Gregg Snyder

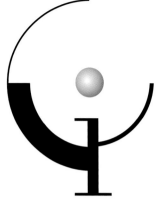

Client:
Innovision
Nature of Business:
Health care systems providers
Design Firm:
Esser Design Inc.
Art Director:
Steve Esser
Designer:
Steve Esser
Illustrator:
Steve Esser

INNOVISION

Client:
Northwestern University, Kellogg
Graduate School of Management
Nature of Business:
Asian business conference
Design Firm:
Michael Stanard, Inc.
Art Director:
Michael Stanard
Designer:
Deb Homsi
Illustrator:
Deb Homsi

Client:
US WEST
Design Firm:
Vaughn Wedeen Creative
Art Director:
Steve Wedeen
Designers:
Lucy Hitchcock, Adabel Kaskiewicz
Illustrator:
Vivian Harder

Client:
US WEST
Design Firm:
Vaughn Wedeen Creative
Art Directors:
Steve Wedeen, Rick Vaughn
Designers:
Steve Wedeen, Rick Vaughn

Client:
Pulaski County Public Library
Nature of Business:
Library
Design Firm:
Kirby Stephens Design Inc.
Art Director:
Kirby Stephens
Designer:
Bill Jones

Client:
NewTech Fiber Optics
Design Firm:
Sibley/Peteet Design, Inc.
Art Director:
Don Sibley
Designer:
Derek Welch

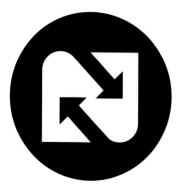

Client:
Pacific Spirit Investment
Management Inc.
Nature of Business:
Investment firm
Design Firm:
Tandem Design Associates Ltd.
Art Director:
Naomi Broudo
Designers:
Violet Finvers, Lesley Casson

Client:
National Park Service
Design Firm:
Clifford Selbert Design
Collaborative
Art Director:
Clifford Selbert
Designer:
Melanie Lowe
Illustrator:
Historical archives
Photographer:
Historical archives

Client:
AIDS Services of New Mexico
Design Firm:
Vaugh Wedeen Creative
Art Directors:
Steve Wedeen, Dan Flynn
Designer:
Dan Flynn
Illustrator:
Vivian Harder

Client:
Leadership Works
Design Firm:
Dale Vermeer Design
Art Director:
Dale Vermeer
Designers:
Dale Vermeer, Cyd Shizuru

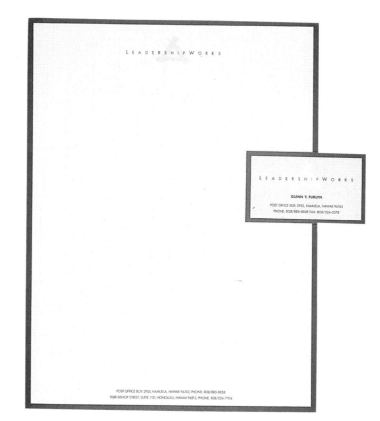

Client:
Synectics International
Design Firm:
Swieter Design United States
Art Director:
John Swieter
Designers:
Mark Ford, John Swieter

Client:
Paris Presents, Inc.
Nature of Business:
Manufacturer of bath and beauty
accessories
Design Firm:
Michael Stanard, Inc.
Art Director:
Michael Stanard
Designer:
Marc C. Fuhrman
Illustrator:
Marc C. Fuhrman

Client:
Shawnee Mills
Nature of Business:
Producer of cattlefeed, flour,
and cake mix
Design Firm:
Sibley/Peteet Design, Inc.
Art Director:
Rex Peteet
Designer:
Tom Hough

Client:
Synectics International
Nature of Business:
Data services consultants
Design Firm:
Swieter Design United States
Art Director:
John Swieter
Designer:
Mark Ford

Client:
California Center for the Arts,
Escondido
Design Firm:
Mires Design, Inc.
Art Director:
John Ball
Designer:
John Ball

Client:
City of Melbourne, Victoria,
Australia
Design Firm:
FHA Image Design
Art Directors:
Richard Henderson, Trevor Flett
Designers:
Keith Smith, Julia Jarvis

Client:
Christiansen, Fritsch, Giersdorf,
Grant & Sperry, Inc. (Cf2GS)
Design Firm:
Hornall Anderson
Design Works, Inc.
Art Director:
Jack Anderson
Designers:
Jack Anderson, David Bates,
Cliff Chung

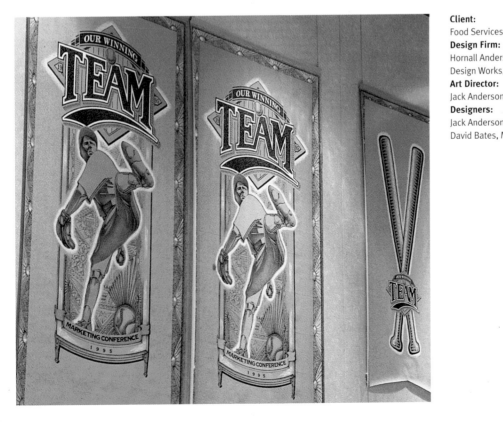

Client:
Food Services of America
Design Firm:
Hornall Anderson
Design Works, Inc.
Art Director:
Jack Anderson
Designers:
Jack Anderson, Cliff Chung,
David Bates, Mary Hermes

Client:
Sojourn
Nature of Business:
Haircare products manufacturer
Design Firm:
Anderson Jones Partners
Art Director:
Scott Marsh
Designer:
Scott Marsh

Client:
Sweeping Changes, Inc.
Nature of Business:
Broom manufacturing company
Design Firm:
Michael Stanard, Inc.
Art Director:
Michael Stanard

Client:
V-Comp Limited
Nature of Business:
Computer systems consultant
Design Firm:
Telmet Design Associates
Art Director:
Tiit Telmet
Designers:
Joseph Gault, Tiit Telmet
Illustrator:
Joseph Gault

Client:
Vitria Technology, Inc.
Nature of Business:
Systems management consulting
Design Firm:
Earl Gee Design
Art Directors:
Earl Gee, Fani Chung
Designers:
Earl Gee, Fani Chung
Illustrator:
Earl Gee

Client:
West 2nd Real Estate
Nature of Business:
Real estate agency
Design Firm:
Tandem Design Associates, Ltd.
Art Director:
Naomi Broudo
Designer:
Violet Finvers

Client:
XactData Corporation
Nature of Business:
System back-up provider
Design Firm:
Hornall Anderson
Design Works, Inc.
Art Director:
Jack Anderson
Designers:
Jack Anderson, Jana Wilson,
Lisa Cerveny, Julie Keenan

Client:
Deleo Clay Tile Co.
Design Firm:
Mires Design, Inc.
Art Directors:
José Serrano
Designer:
José Serrano
Illustrators:
Nancy Stahl,
Tracy Sabin

Client:
Australian Department of
Employment Education & Training
Design Firm:
FHA Image Design
Art Director:
Trevor Flett
Designer:
Lee McCartney

Client:
Caledonian, Inc.
Design Firm:
Michael Stanard, Inc.
Art Director:
Michael Stanard
Designer:
Lisa Fingerhut
Illustrator:
Lisa Fingerhut

Client:
Kirima Design Office
Design Firm:
Kirima Design Office
Art Director:
Harumi Kirima
Designer:
Harumi Kirima
Photographer:
Akifumi Ishii

Client:
Wildfire Communications
Design Firm:
Clifford Selbert Design
Collaborative
Art Director:
Robin Perkins
Designer:
Stephanie Wade

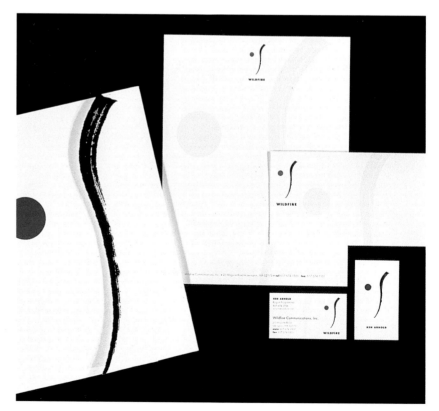

Client:
Motorola
Design Firm:
Vaughn Wedeen Creative
Art Directors:
Steve Wedeen, Dan Flynn
Designer:
Dan Flynn
Photographer:
Stephen Marks

Client:
Raleigh Paper
Design Firm:
Harcus Design
Art Director:
Annette Harcus
Designers:
Kristin Thieme, Annette Harcus
Illustrator:
Kristin Thieme

Client:
Eye to Eye Creative Solutions
Nature of Business:
Video producer
Design Firm:
Ron Kellum, Inc.
Designers:
Ron Kellum, Beverly McClain

Client:
Latent Image Photography
Nature of Business:
Photography studio
Design Firm:
PPA Design Limited
Art Director:
Byron Jacobs
Designer:
Byron Jacobs

Client:
Copeland Reis Agency
Nature of Business:
Talent agency
Design Firm:
Mires Design, Inc.
Art Director:
John Ball
Designer:
John Ball

Client:
US WEST Foundation
Design Firm:
Vaughn Wedeen Creative
Art Director:
Steve Wedeen
Designer:
Steve Wedeen
Illustrator:
Vivian Harder

Client:
Frank Russell Company
Design Firm:
Hornall Anderson
Design Works, Inc.
Art Director:
Jack Anderson
Designers:
Jack Anderson, Lisa Cerveny,
Suzanne Haddon

Client:
Made On Earth
Design Firm:
Jay Vigon Studio
Art Director:
Jay Vigon
Designer:
Jay Vigon

Client:
Natural Cycle Club
Design Firm:
Jay Vigon Studio
Art Director:
Jay Vigon
Designer:
Jay Vigon

NISACT

Client:
NISACT
Nature of Business:
Translingual communications
Design Firm:
X Design Co.
Art Director:
Alex Valderrama
Designer:
Alex Valderrama
Illustrator:
Alex Valderrama

Client:
TKO Graphics, Inc.
Nature of Business:
Multimedia design firm
Design Firm:
TKO Graphics, Inc.
Art Director:
Tom Gavel
Designer:
Ralph Miolla

Client:
DART Transit Police
Nature of Business:
Transit police
Design Firm:
Swieter Design United States
Art Director:
John Swieter
Designer:
Kevin Flatt

Client:
30Sixty Design, Inc.
Design Firm:
30Sixty Design, Inc.
Art Director:
Henry Vizcarra
Designer:
Brian Lane

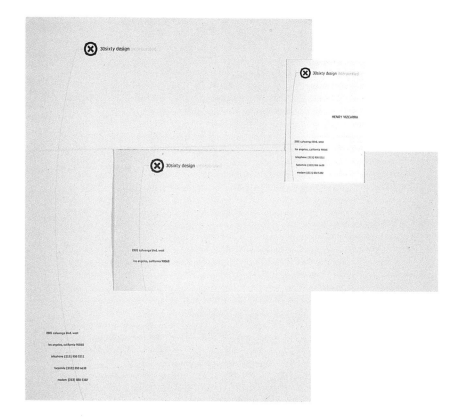

Client:
ID, Inc.
Design Firm:
ID, Inc.
Art Director:
Robert Aughenbaugh
Designers:
Jonathan Mulcare, Dru Martin

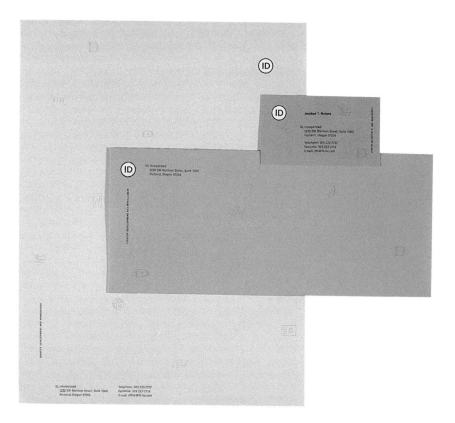

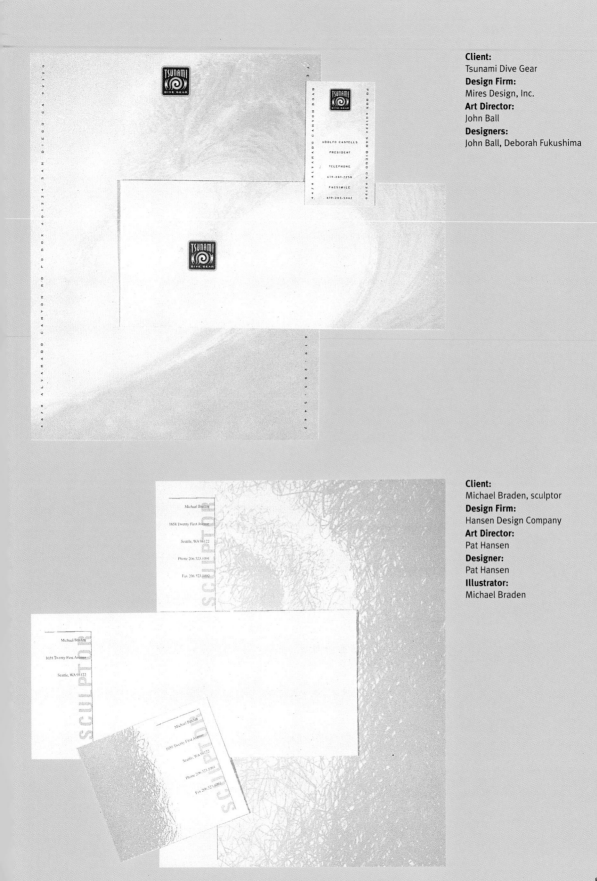

Client:
Tsunami Dive Gear
Design Firm:
Mires Design, Inc.
Art Director:
John Ball
Designers:
John Ball, Deborah Fukushima

Client:
Michael Braden, sculptor
Design Firm:
Hansen Design Company
Art Director:
Pat Hansen
Designer:
Pat Hansen
Illustrator:
Michael Braden

Client:
African American Museum
Nature of Business:
Museum
Design Firm:
RBMM/The Richards Group
Designer:
Luis D. Acevedo
Illustrator:
Wayne Johnson

Client:
A3 Architects
Nature of Business:
Architectural firm
Design Firm:
Harcus Design
Art Director:
Annette Harcus
Designer:
Annette Harcus

Client:
Commercial Furniture Interiors
Nature of Business:
Furniture designers
Design Firm:
Toni Schowalter Design
Art Director:
Toni Schowalter
Designer:
Toni Schowalter

Client:
Telogy
Design Firm:
Michael Patrick Partners
Art Director:
Duane Maidens
Designers:
Bernie Wooster, Roy Tazuma,
Alle Ashton
Photographer:
Jiles Hancock

Client:
Starbucks Coffee Company
Design Firm:
Hornall Anderson
Design Works, Inc.
Art Director:
Jack Anderson
Designers:
Jack Anderson, Mary Chin
Hutchison, Julie Lock,
Bruce Branson-Meyer
Illustrator:
Julia LaPine

Client:
Sazaby, Inc.
Design Firm:
Matsumoto Incorporated
Art Director:
Takaaki Matsumoto
Designer:
Takaaki Matsumoto

Client:
Estée Lauder
Design Firm:
Clifford Selbert Design
Collaborative
Art Director:
Clifford Selbert
Designer:
Melanie Lowe

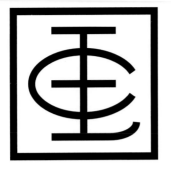

I.C.L. by SAZABY

Client:
Sazaby, Inc.
Nature of Business:
Retail corporation
Design Firm:
Matsumoto Incorporated
Art Director:
Takaaki Matsumoto
Designer:
Takaaki Matsumoto

Client:
Felissimo Universal Corporation
of the Orient Ltd.
Nature of Business:
Brand of cosmetics
Design Firm:
Kirima Design Office
Art Director:
Harumi Kirima
Designer:
Fumitaka Yukawa

Client:
Luis Mejid
Nature of Business:
Architect
Design Firm:
RBMM/The Richards Group
Art Director:
Horacio Cobos
Designer:
Horacio Cobos
Illustrator:
Horacio Cobos

Client:
Monika Hummer Design
Nature of Business:
Freelance graphic designer
Design Firm:
Monika Hummer Design
Designer:
Monika Hummer

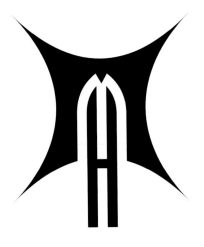

Client:
Mark Watson Building
& Renovation
Nature of Business:
Construction company
Design Firm:
Jerry Takigawa Design
Art Director:
Jerry Takigawa
Designer:
Glenn Johnson
Illustrator:
Glenn Johnson

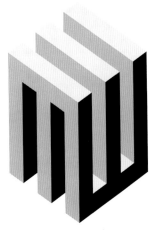

Client:
Onkyo
Nature of Business:
Electronic equipment manufacturer
Design Firm:
Hornall Anderson
Design Works, Inc.
Art Director:
Jack Anderson
Designers:
Jack Anderson, Lisa Cerveny,
David Bates

Client:
Meltzer & Martin
Design Firm:
SullivanPerkins
Art Director:
Andrea Peterson
Designer:
Andrea Peterson

Client:
Thirstype
Design Firm:
ForDesign
Art Directors:
Frank Ford, Rick Valicenti
Designer:
Frank Ford
Illustrator:
Frank Ford

Client:
Plus Q Co., Ltd.
Nature of Business:
Editors and publishers
Design Firm:
Packaging Create
Art Director:
Akio Okumura
Designer:
Emi Kajihara

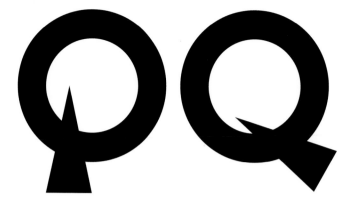

Client:
Saint Luke's Episcopal Church
Nature of Business:
Church
Design Firm:
Weller Institute for the Cure
of Design
Art Director:
Don Weller
Designer:
Don Weller
Illustrator:
Don Weller

SAINT LUKE'S
EPISCOPAL CHURCH

Client:
DFS Group Limited
Nature of Business:
Duty-free shop
Design Firm:
Sackett Design Associates
Art Director:
Mark Sackett
Designers:
Mark Sackett, Wayne Sakamoto
Illustrator:
Wayne Sakamoto

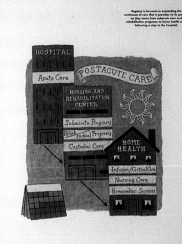

To our
Shareholders:

The year just ended, 1994, was a watershed year for Regency Health Services and its shareholders. In April, it merged with Care Enterprises, making the combined entity the dominant long-term and specialty health care provider in California, and establishing for Regency, a presence in New Mexico, Ohio and West Virginia. Today Regency operates through 94 facilities with 9,274 beds. The assimilation process of the merger, and perhaps the rapid growth over the past two years, proved more difficult to digest than anticipated, and earnings for the second quarter dropped significantly from projections. At all levels of the company considerable effort has been focused on improving operations, increasing revenue, and controlling costs.

The result of our efforts is reflected in the quarter-to-quarter growth in after-tax operating income per share, excluding non-recurring items, rising from $0.12 in the second quarter, to $0.15 in the third quarter, and to $0.18 in the fourth quarter. Our occupancy rate in the fourth quarter increased to 92.7% compared with 92.1% in the third quarter and with 91.2% in the second quarter. We expect our financial results to reflect continued improvement throughout 1995.

Revenues for 1994 were $380.9 million compared with $340.9 million for 1993. After-tax income from operations for 1994, excluding merger and restructuring charges and an extraordinary item related to the California earthquake in January 1994 was $10.8 million, or $0.63 per share. Net income in 1993 was $11.7 million, or $0.69 per share. Including the non-recurring items, the company reported a net loss in 1994 of $(0.8) million, or $(0.05) per share.

Building for the Future During 1994, we took important steps to provide Regency with critical competitive advantages in the evolving marketplace for long-term and specialty health care services.

Regency Health Services

94

Client:
Regency Health Service
Design Firm:
Baker Design Associates
Art Director:
Gary Robert Baker
Designer:
Yee-Ping Cho
Illustrator:
James Steinberg
Photographers:
Marc Carter, Scott Robinson

When I scream *Eureka!* or perhaps *Yutzga!*
the world will welcome a new word
which was born
in the house of the mind and the heart.

I finally plop down on a cushy couch
with a stack of books.
It has started to rain outside.
I will be here for hours
asking solicitous people
wearing thesauruses
to bring me books, bring me snacks,
bring me more paper, more pens.

This will be an epic night.

Client:
Barnes & Noble, Inc.
Design Firm:
Kiku Obata & Company
Art Directors:
Joe Floresca, Kiku Obata
Designer:
Joe Floresca
Illustrator:
Maira Kalman

Client:
Amnesty International Australia
Design Firm:
Y's Communication
Creative Director:
Phil Young
Designer:
Simon Fuentes

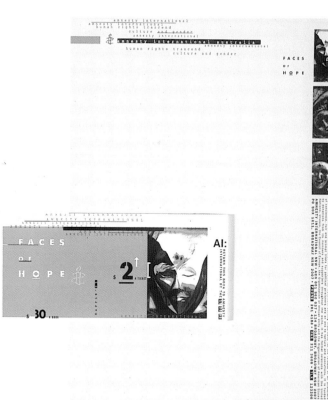

Client:
Pronto Reproduction
Design Firm:
Telmet Design Associates
Art Director:
Tiit Telmet
Designer:
Robert Farrell

Client:
Clifford Selbert Design
Collaborative
Design Firm:
Clifford Selbert Design
Collaborative
Art Director:
Darren Namaye
Designer:
Darren Namaye

Client:
Premier Rôle agent
Design Firm:
Tarzan Communications, Inc.
Art Directors:
George Fok, Daniel Fortin
Designers:
George Fok, Daniel Fortin

Client:
Bremer Jewelry
Nature of Business:
Jeweler
Design Firm:
Simantel Group
Art Director:
Wendy Behrens
Designer:
Lisa Vanden Eynden

Client:
Duo Delights
Nature of Business:
Line of dessert sauces
and brownie mixes
Design Firm:
Lambert Design Studio
Art Director:
Christie Lambert
Designer:
Joy Cathey Price
Illustrator:
Joy Cathey Price

Client:
Mission Ridge
Nature of Business:
Ski resort
Design Firm:
Hornall Anderson
Design Works, Inc.
Art Director:
Jack Anderson
Designers:
Jack Anderson, Cliff Chung,
Denise Weir, David Bates,
Leo Raymundo
Letterer:
George Tanagi

BREMER J E W E L R Y

Client:
Bremer Jewelry
Nature of Business:
Jeweler
Design Firm:
Simantel Group
Art Director:
Wendy Behrens
Designer:
Lisa Vanden Eynden

cuRio

Client:
David Lemon, Curio Ensemble
Nature of Business:
Chamber music performance group
Design Firm:
Signals Design Group, Inc.
Art Director:
Kosta (Gus) Tsetsekas
Designers:
Kosta (Gus) Tsetsekas,
Nando De Girolamo
Illustrator:
Nando De Girolamo

G O O D D O G S

Client:
DooKim Design
Design Firm:
DooKim Design
Art Director:
Doo H. Kim
Designers:
Dongil Lee, Seung Hee Lee

Client:
O & J Design, Inc.
Design Firm:
O & J Design, Inc.
Art Director:
Andrzej J. Olejniczak
Designers:
Andrew Jablonski,
Inhi Clara Kim,
Andrzej J. Olejniczak,
Lia Camara-Mariscal

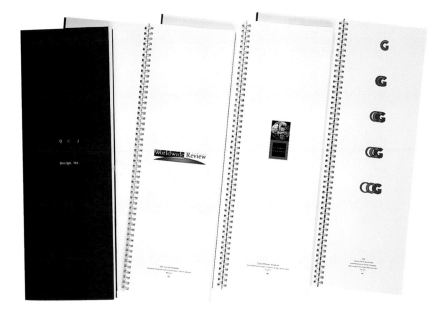

Client:
Fox Broadcasting Company
Design Firm:
30Sixty Design Inc.
Art Director:
Henry Vizcarra
Designer:
Pär Larsson
Photographer:
Scott Hensel

Client:
Bonesteel Productions
Nature of Business:
Documentary film studio
Design Firm:
Critt Graham & Associates
Art Director:
Gregg Snyder
Designer:
Gregg Snyder

Client:
Top Dogs Productions
Nature of Business:
Photography studio
Design Firm:
RBMM/The Richards Group
Art Director:
Pamela Chang
Designer:
Pamela Chang
Illustrator:
Pamela Chang

Client:
DogStar Design
Nature of Business:
Graphic design studio
Design Firm:
DogStar Design
Designer:
Rodney Davidson
Illustrator:
Rodney Davidson

Client:
The Buffalo Connection
Nature of Business:
Restaurant
Design Firm:
DogStar Design
Designer:
Rodney Davidson
Illustrator:
Rodney Davidson

Client:
Wolf Mechanics
Nature of Business:
Machine shop
Design Firm:
RBMM/The Richards Group
Art Director:
Ken Shafer
Designer:
Shayne Washburn
Illustrator:
Shayne Washburn

Client:
NFL Properties
Nature of Business:
Sports merchandiser
Design Firm:
Sean Michael Edward Design
Art Director:
Ed O'Hara
Designer:
Andrew Blanco
Illustrator:
Andrew Blanco

Client:
Paradise Wild
Nature of Business:
Nature-related retailer
Design Firm:
Supon Design Group
Art Director:
Andrew Dolan
Designer:
Andrew Dolan
Illustrator:
Andrew Dolan

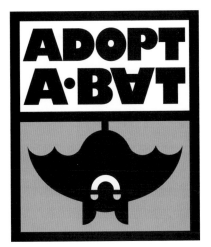

Client:
Adopt-A-Bat
Nature of Business:
Bat conservation organization
Design Firm:
Sibley/Peteet Design, Inc.
Art Director:
Rex Peteet
Designer:
Rex Peteet
Illustrator:
Rex Peteet

Client:
S. D. Johnson Company
Nature of Business:
Line of fishing products
Design Firm:
Mires Design, Inc.
Art Director:
John Ball
Designer:
John Ball
Illustrator:
Tracy Sabin

Client:
Pacific Corporation
Design Firm:
DooKim Design
Art Director:
Doo H. Kim
Designer:
Dongil Lee, Seung Hee Lee

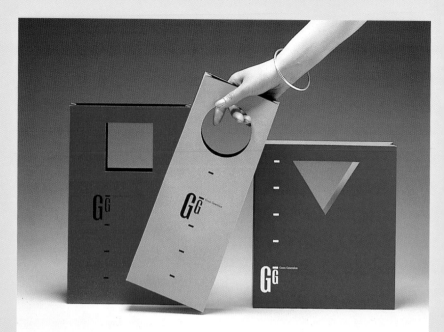

Client:
Nordstrom Factory Direct
Design Firm:
Hornall Anderson
Design Works, Inc.
Art Director:
Jack Anderson
Designers:
Jack Anderson, David Bates,
Cliff Chung

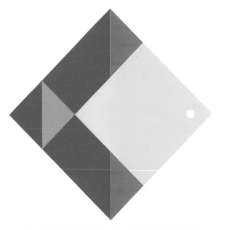

CINCINNATI AQUARIUM

Client:
Cincinnati Aquarium
Nature of Business:
Aquarium
Design Firm:
The Benchmark Group
Designer:
John Carpenter

AWASHIMA HOTEL

Client:
Awashima Island Resort
Nature of Business:
Island Resort
Design Firm:
Matsumoto Incorporated
Art Director:
Takaaki Matsumoto
Designer:
Takaaki Matsumoto

Client:
Sea Science Center
Nature of Business:
Aquatic Museum
Design Firm:
DogStar Design
Art Director:
George Fuller
Designer:
Rodney Davidson
Illustrator:
Rodney Davidson

Client:
Waterfront Regeneration Trust
Design Firm:
Scott Thornley & Co.
Art Director:
Scott Thornley
Designers:
Henry Zaluski, Bruce Aitken

Client:
SkiView
Nature of Business:
Ski resort advertising network
Design Firm:
John Brady Design Consultants, Inc.
Art Director:
Mona MacDonald
Designer:
Rick Madison
Illustrator:
Rick Madison

Client:
SeaVision
Nature of Business:
Developer of cruise television
Design Firm:
John Brady Design Consultants, Inc.
Art Director:
John Brady
Designer:
Rick Madison
Illustrator:
Rick Madison

MAD COW FARMS

Client:
Mad Cow Farms
Nature of Business:
Horse training farm
Design Firm:
Simantel Group
Art Director:
Lisa Vanden Eynden
Designer:
Lisa Vanden Eynden

Client:
Timbuktuu Coffee Bar
Nature of Business:
Coffeehouse
Design Firm:
Sayles Graphic Design
Art Director:
John Sayles
Designer:
John Sayles
Illustrator:
John Sayles

Client:
DogStar Design
Nature of Business:
Studio's pro bono work
Design Firm:
DogStar Design
Designer:
Rodney Davidson
Illustrator:
Rodney Davidson

TIDBITS

LEFT

Client:
Okamoto Corporation
Design Firm:
Hornall Anderson
Design Works, Inc.
Art Director:
John Hornall
Designers:
John Hornall, Julie Lock,
Mary Hermes, Julie Keenan

RIGHT

Client:
Innovision
Design Firm:
Esser Design Inc.
Art Directors:
Steve Esser, Pam Esser
Designer:
Jodi Goll
Illustrator:
Steve Musgrave
Photographer:
Bill Timmerman

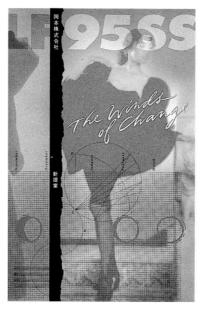

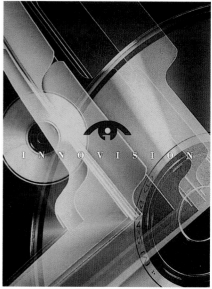

LEFT

Client:
Lasertechnics, Inc.
Design Firm:
Vaughn Wedeen Creative
Art Director:
Steve Wedeen
Designers:
Steve Wedeen, Adabel Kaskiewicz
Photographer:
Dave Nufer

RIGHT

Client:
BRC Imagination Arts
Design Firm:
30Sixty Design Inc.
Art Director:
Henry Vizcarra
Designer:
Brian Lane
Photographers:
Scott Hensel, Jeff Simon

A second reason to be optimistic about our Laser Marking Division is the positive response we have received to Xymark, a new coding laser that we are exclusively marketing in the United States for Coherent Hull, Ltd., its British manufacturer. Simply put, X...

our

Letter from The Office of the Chairman

Dear Shareholders,

Lasertechnics took a firm new direction in 1992. The Board of Directors appointed Eugene A. Bourque as President and created a special management committee to oversee operations. It is comprised of Bourque, Chairman of the Board and CEO Richard M. Clarke, and Vice Chairman Harrison H. Schmitt. These ... were made after the resignation ... former president

Lasertechnics Annual Report 1992

Lasertechnics designs,
manufactures and market...
laser coding system...
digital laser pr...
use in indust...
...to maximi...
value i...
reflec...
conmer...
by c...

committee
...orts of all
... on what the
...went back to
...our lease obliga-
...ornia facility, and
...products that had
...eir productive life
...our Fizeau wave-
... we had sold for
...rs, was not selling
...ucts with lower
...discontinued it.
...the technology and
...n our beam directed
...ch Electro-Optics, Inc.,
...pany. Furthermore, we
...he refurbishing business
...5000, and concentrated

back
to
basics

[a dramatic new direction]

Client:
Lasertechnics, Inc.
Design Firm:
Vaughn Wedeen Creative
Art Director:
Steve Wedeen
Designer:
Steve Wedeen

Client:
A Planet Called Earth
Nature of Business:
Environmental retail store
Design Firm:
Supon Design Group
Art Directors:
Andrew Dolan, Supon Phornirunlit
Designer:
Deborah N. Savitt
Illustrator:
Deborah N. Savitt

Client:
Supon Design Group
Nature of Business:
Graphic design firm
Design Firm:
Supon Design Group
Art Directors:
Andrew Dolan, Supon Phornirunlit
Designer:
David Carroll
Illustrator:
David Carroll

Client:
Amerifest Dallas (Texas)
Nature of Business:
Civic festival
Design Firm:
RBMM/The Richards Group
Art Director:
Horacio Cobos
Designer:
Horacio Cobos
Illustrators:
Horacio Cobos, Wayne Johnson

Banyule

Client:
Banyule (Victoria, Australia)
City Council
Nature of Business:
Civil government
Design Firm:
Blizzard Allen Creative Services
Art Director:
Anthony Coombes
Designer:
Anthony Coombes
Illustrator:
Anthony Coombes

Client:
Brittany Hartly
Nature of Business:
Ballerina
Design Firm:
Sibley/Peteet Design
Art Director:
Mark Brinkman
Designer:
Mark Brinkman

Client:
Capons Rotisserie Chicken
Nature of Business:
Restaurant chain
Design Firm:
Hornall Anderson
Design Works, Inc.
Art Director:
Jack Anderson
Designers:
Jack Anderson, David Bates
Illustrators:
David Bates, George Tanagi

Client:
Chemical Bank
Nature of Business:
Financial institution
Design Firm:
Sayles Graphic Design
Art Director:
John Sayles
Designer:
John Sayles
Illustrator:
John Sayles

Client:
Hawk's Nest Publishing
Nature of Business:
In-house publisher for
elementary school
Design Firm:
Lambert Design Studio
Art Director:
Christie Lambert
Designer:
Joy Cathey Price

Client:
Non-no Co., Ltd.
Nature of Business:
Clothing company
Design Firm:
DooKim Design
Art Director:
Doo H. Kim
Designers:
Dongil Lee, Seung Hee Lee

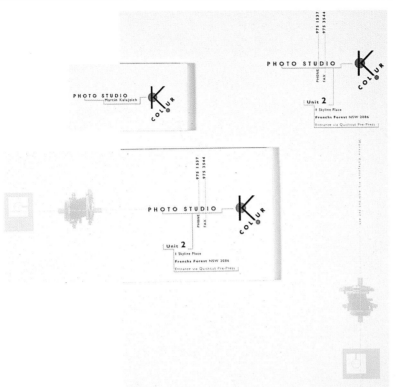

Client:
K Colour Photo Studio
Design Firm:
Y's Communication
Creative Director:
Phil Young
Designer:
Simon Fuentes

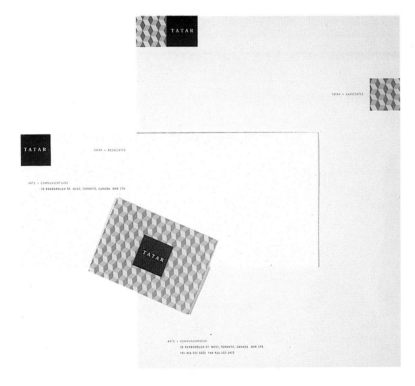

Client:
Judith Tatar
Design Firm:
Concrete Design Communications
Inc., Toronto
Art Directors:
John Pylypczak, Diti Katona
Designers:
Susan McIntee, Diti Katona

Client:
Horse Power Couriers
Nature of Business:
Messenger service
Design Firm:
Sibley/Peteet Design, Inc.
Art Director:
Derek Welch
Designer:
Derek Welch
Illustrator:
Derek Welch

Client:
Los Arcos Mall
Nature of Business:
Shopping center
Design Firm:
Sibley/Peteet Design, Inc.
Art Directors:
David Beck, Rex Peteet
Designer:
David Beck
Illustrator:
David Beck

Client:
Turtle Creek Run
Nature of Business:
Residential development
Design Firm:
Sibley/Peteet Design, Inc.
Art Director:
Derek Welch
Designer:
Derek Welch
Illustrator:
Derek Welch

Client:
Birmingham (Alabama)
Junior League
Nature of Business:
Inner-city reading project
Design Firm:
DogStar Design
Art Director:
Tracy Brabner
Designer:
Rodney Davidson
Illustrator:
Rodney Davidson

BLACK SCORPION™

Client:
MerCruiser
Nature of Business:
Tournament in-board
ski engines company
Design Firm:
SHR Perceptual Management
Art Director:
Mike Barton
Illustrator:
13th Floor

Client:
EnerShop
Nature of Business:
Energy roundup convention
Design Firm:
Sibley/Peteet Design, Inc.
Art Director:
Rex Peteet
Designer:
Derek Welch
Illustrator:
Derek Welch

Client:
Potomac Conference of S.D.A.
Nature of Business:
Young scientists expo
Design Firm:
Alphawave Designs
Art Director:
Douglas Dunbebin
Designer:
Douglas Dunbebin
Illustrator:
Douglas Dunbebin

Client:
Hart's Fitness Center
Nature of Business:
Health club
Design Firm:
Sibley/Peteet Design, Inc.
Art Director:
Rex Peteet
Designer:
Derek Welch
Illustrator:
Derek Welch

Client:
A Meacham Creative
Nature of Business:
Advertising and public relations
company
Design Firm:
Sayles Graphic Design
Art Director:
John Sayles
Designer:
John Sayles
Illustrator:
John Sayles

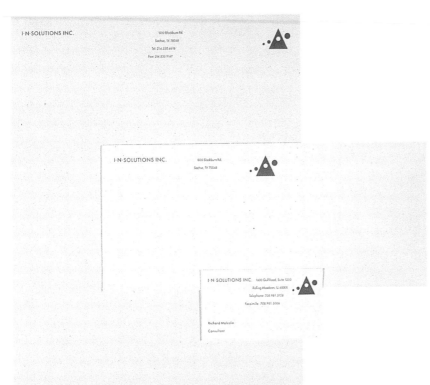

Client:
IN SOLUTIONS
Design Firm:
Peterson & Company
Art Director:
Scott Ray
Designer:
Scott Ray
Illustrator:
Scott Ray

Client:
Innovative Thinking Conference
Design Firm:
SHR Perceptual Management
Art Director:
Barry Shepard
Designer:
Nathan Joseph

INNOVATIVE THINKING CONFERENCE 5

INNOVATIVE THINKING CONFERENCE 5

8700 E. Via de Ventura, Suite 100
Scottsdale, AZ 85258 USA

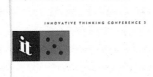

8700 E. Via de Ventura, Suite 100
Scottsdale, AZ 85258 USA
Telephone 602.443.7431
Fax 602.483.9675

Client:
Arlington (Texas) Museum of Art
Nature of Business:
Art museum
Design Firm:
Swieter Design United States
Art Director:
John Swieter
Designer:
Jenice Heo

Client:
Mahlum & Nordfors McKinley
Gordon
Nature of Business:
Architectural firm
Design Firm:
Hornall Anderson
Design Works, Inc.
Art Director:
Jack Anderson
Designers:
Jack Anderson, Leo Raymundo,
Scott Eggers

Client:
National Museum of Australia
Nature of Business:
"A Changing People—A Changing
Land" exhibit
Design Firm:
Spatchurst Design Associates
Art Director:
John Spatchurst
Illustrator:
John Spatchurst

P R A I X S

Client:
Praxis Group
Nature of Business:
Consulting firm
Design Firm:
Weller Institute for
the Cure of Design
Art Director:
Don Weller
Designer:
Don Weller
Illustrator:
Don Weller

Client:
Shower Heads Shampoo
Nature of Business:
Shampoo maker
Design Firm:
Swieter Design United States
Art Director:
John Swieter
Designer:
Paul Munsterman

CYKO

Client:
Cyko, Inc.
Nature of Business:
Wheel manufacturer
Design Firm:
X Design Company
Art Director:
Alex Valderrama
Designer:
Alex Valderrama
Illustrator:
Alex Valderrama

Client:
Riverview Dining Room
Design Firm:
Harcus Design
Art Director:
Annette Harcus
Designers:
Lucy Walker, Annette Harcus
Illustrator:
Annette Harcus

Client:
Target Stores
Design Firm:
Hedstrom/Blessing
Art Director:
Mike Goebel
Designer:
Mike Goebel

The Sunday Club

Client:
The Sunday Club
Nature of Business:
Social club
Design Firm:
Pictogram Studio
Art Director:
Stephanie Hooton
Designer:
Hien Nguyen
Illustrator:
Hien Nguyen

Client:
The Sunday Club
Nature of Business:
Social club (biking)
Design Firm:
Pictogram Studio
Art Director:
Stephanie Hooton
Designer:
Hien Nguyen
Illustrator:
Hien Nguyen

Client:
The Sunday Club
Nature of Business:
Social club (skating)
Design Firm:
Pictogram Studio
Art Director:
Stephanie Hooton
Designer:
Hien Nguyen
Illustrator:
Hien Nguyen

Client:
Ellen Knable & Associates
Nature of Business:
Artist's representative
Design Firm:
Jay Vigon Studio
Art Director:
Jay Vigon
Designer:
Jay Vigon

Client:
Matthews Media Group
Nature of Business:
Financial trust program
Design Firm:
Alphawave Designs
Art Director:
Douglas Dunbebin
Designer:
Douglas Dunbebin
Illustrator:
Douglas Dunbebin

Client:
Konrad Bright
Nature of Business:
Personal tattoo
Design Firm:
Bright & Associates
Art Director:
Konrad Bright
Designer:
Konrad Bright
Illustrator:
Konrad Bright

Client:
Dr. Raul E. Varela
Nature of Business:
Joint and muscle medicine practice
Design Firm:
Varela Graphics
Art Director:
Raul Varela
Designer:
Raul Varela

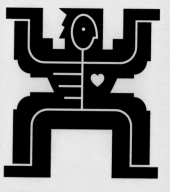

Client:
Charles James
Nature of Business:
Personal fitness trainer
Design Firm:
Sibley/Peteet Design, Inc.
Art Director:
David Beck
Designer:
David Beck
Illustrators:
David Beck, Mike Broshous

Client:
Inquisition Software
Nature of Business:
Software company
Design Firm:
Sayles Graphic Design
Art Director:
John Sayles
Designer:
John Sayles
Illustrator:
John Sayles

Client:
Carelinc/The Porter Group
Nature of Business:
Management consulting group
Design Firm:
Sackett Design Associates
Art Director:
Mark Sackett
Designers:
Mark Sackett, Clark Richardson
Illustrator:
Clark Richardson

Client:
National Association of
Independent Schools
Nature of Business:
Conference
Design Firm:
Dever Designs, Inc.
Art Director:
Jeffrey Dever
Designer:
Emily Kendall

Client:
Lord Howe Island Board
Nature of Business:
Cultivator/exporter of palm trees
native to Lord Howe Island
Design Firm:
Harcus Design
Art Director:
Annette Harcus
Designers:
Annette Harcus, Lucy Walker
Illustrator:
Annette Harcus

Client:
Hanley-Wood, Inc.
Design Firm:
William J. Kircher & Associates, Inc.
Art Director:
Bruce E. Morgan
Designer:
Bruce E. Morgan

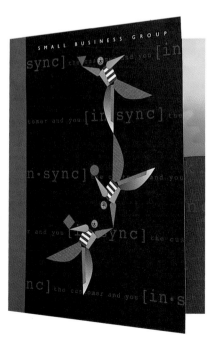

LEFT
Client:
US WEST
Design Firm:
Vaughn Wedeen Creative
Art Director:
Rick Vaughn
Designer:
Rick Vaughn
Illustrator:
Rick Vaughn
Photographer:
Michael Barley

RIGHT
Client:
San Francisco Film Society
Design Firm:
Primo Angeli, Inc.
Art Directors:
Primo Angeli, Carlo Pagoda
Designer:
Primo Angeli
Computer Illustrator:
Marcelo De Freitas
Production Manager:
Eric Kubly

Client:
Horizon Healthcare

Design Firm:
Vaughn Wedeen Creative

Art Directors:
Rick Vaughn, Dan Flynn

Designer:
Dan Flynn

Illustrator:
Greg Tucker

Corp. (NRS) now provide comprehensive therapy services through 276 contracts, covering approximately 31,000 beds – a 71 percent increase in beds served over the prior fiscal year.

During fiscal 1994, growth was concentrated in Ohio, Florida, Colorado, Texas and Connecticut. We also integrated certain therapists from the Greenery facilities into the Horizon family of companies. Six hundred licensed therapists now provide quality physical, occupational, speech, respiratory and ventilator therapy. These CRC and NRS professionals are dedicated to providing quality care that enables patients to achieve a higher quality of life by living at their highest level of functional ability. For managed care providers, HMOs and other payors, rehabilitation therapy services offer cost effective outcomes – a necessity in the delivery of affordable health care.

Looking ahead, we are committed to aggressive expansion of our rehabilitation division, both through acquisitions and internal growth. Additionally, we will

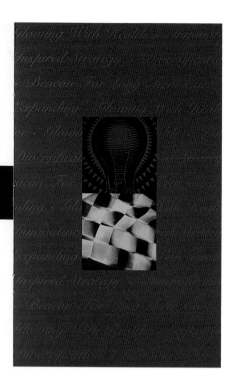

OUR PROVEN ABILITY TO ACQUIRE LONG TERM CARE CENTERS AND INTEGRATE OUR SPECIALTY SERVICES WILL CONTINUE AS WE EXPAND OUR BUSINESS 15-20 PERCENT PER YEAR DURING THE NEXT SEVERAL YEARS.

market new contracts to non-affiliated long-term care providers, hospitals, school systems, outpatient clinics and other sources.

PHARMACY

Fiscal 1994 was a year of significant growth for National Institutional Pharmacy Services, Inc., (NIPSI), our wholly owned institutional pharmacy subsidiary. Through our 14 pharmacies, we now provide a full range of pharmaceutical, infusion therapy and enteral and parenteral nutritional therapy products and services to facilities operated by Horizon and other long-term care providers in 12 states. We now serve 29,000 beds, a 32 percent increase over last year. Net revenues from NIPSI grew to $27.3 million, a 146 percent increase over the prior year. Our consultant pharmacists provide clinical pharmacy consulting through a standardized computer system for patient charts, review of medication administration and regulation compliance as well as inventory management.

eight

Client:
Six Sigma

Design Firm:
Hornall Anderson
Design Works, Inc.

Art Director:
Jack Anderson

Designers:
Jack Anderson, Bruce Branson-Meyer, Heidi Favour

Photographer:
Tom Collicott

Assembly

*W*ell trained, conscientious teams perform the critical hands-on task of custom assembly. From CDs to manuals, videos and brochures, each product must be precisely collated and packaged with all the correct elements in perfect sequence. Our quality control

THE ART OF

processes guarantee that each completely assembled product has been carefully evaluated at numerous stages by both the tools of technology and the discerning human eye. No compromises. By the time your customers receive their product, we're certain that they will find it in virtually perfect order.

Client:
NFL Properties
Nature of Business:
Sport teams organization
Design Firm:
Evenson Design Group
Art Director:
Stan Evenson
Designer:
Ken Loh

Client:
Japan Package Design Association
Design Firm:
Kirima Design Office
Art Director:
Harumi Kirima
Designer:
Harumi Kirima

Client:
Nike, Inc.
Nature of Business:
Sportswear manufacturer
Design Firm:
Mires Design, Inc.
Art Directors:
Scott Mires, José Serrano
Designers:
José Serrano, Scott Mires
Illustrator:
Tracy Sabin

Client:
Discovery Communications, Inc.
Nature of Business:
Cable network program
Design Firm:
Supon Design Group
Art Director:
Richard Lee Heffner
Designer:
Andrew Dolan
Illustrator:
Andrew Dolan

Client:
Banzai Spoke-n-Ski
Nature of Business:
Mountain bike race
Design Firm:
McCullough Creative Group, Inc.
Art Director:
Michael Schmalz
Designer:
Michael Schmalz

Client:
Museo de Antropología
Nature of Business:
Anthropological museum
Design Firm:
Félix Beltrán + Asociados
Art Director:
Félix Beltrán
Designer:
Patricia Fuentes

Client:
Pennsylvania State University,
Jazz Club
Nature of Business:
Musical group
Design Firm:
Sommese Design
Art Directors:
Lanny Sommese, Kristin Sommese
Designer:
Kristin Sommese
Illustrator:
Lanny Sommese

Client:
David Goldfoot
Nature of Business:
Self
Design Firm:
Boom Design
Art Director:
Larissa Winterhalter
Designers:
Larissa Winterhalter, Joel Goldfoot

Client:
Ljubljanski sejem
Nature of Business:
Robotics fair
Design Firm:
KROG
Art Director:
Edi Berk
Designer:
Edi Berk

Client:
Vaughn Wedeen Creative
Design Firm:
Vaughn Wedeen Creative
Art Director:
Rick Vaughn
Designer:
Rick Vaughn
Illustrators:
Rick Vaughn, Chip Wyly
Photographer:
Dave Nufer

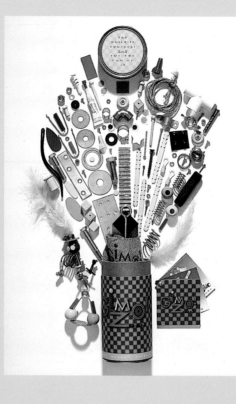

Client:
Twin Palms Restaurant
Design Firm:
McNulty & Company
Art Director:
Jennifer McNulty
Designers:
Jennifer McNulty, Dan McNulty
Illustrator:
Jennifer McNulty

Client:
Pompano Square
Nature of Business:
Retailers
Design Firm:
Tracy Sabin Graphic Design
Art Director:
Tracey Olson
Illustrator:
Tracy Sabin

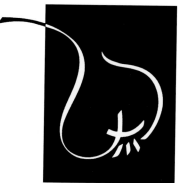

Client:
The Stinking Rose
Nature of Business:
Garlic restaurant
Design Firm:
Second Floor
Art Director:
Warren Welter
Designer:
Carolyn Perot
Illustrator:
Carolyn Perot

Client:
Kirk Alford
Nature of Business:
Piano tuner/technician
Design Firm:
DogStar Design
Designer:
Rodney Davidson
Illustrator:
Rodney Davidson

Client:
Villa Musica
Nature of Business:
Cultural event
Design Firm:
Karl Design
Art Director:
Andreas Karl
Designer:
Andreas Karl
Illustrator:
Andreas Karl

Client:
K. Lee Scott
Nature of Business:
Composer
Design Firm:
DogStar Design
Designer:
Rodney Davidson
Illustrator:
Rodney Davidson

Client:
Gregory Freeze
Nature of Business:
Singer/pianist
Design Firm:
DogStar Design
Designer:
Rodney Davidson
Illustrator:
Rodney Davidson

Client:
Vancouver Recital Society
Nature of Business:
Concert producer
Design Firm:
Signals Design Group, Inc.
Art Director:
Kosta (Gus) Tsetsekas
Designer:
Kosta (Gus) Tsetsekas
Illustrator:
Adam Smith

Client:
First Night State College
Nature of Business:
Annual New Year's Eve celebration
Design Firm:
Sommese Design
Art Director:
Lanny Sommese
Designer:
Kristin Sommese
Illustrator:
Lanny Sommese

Client:
Dewin Tibbs
Nature of Business:
Operatic baritone
Design Firm:
DogStar Design
Designer:
Rodney Davidson
Illustrator:
Rodney Davidson

Client:
Southwest Missouri State
University, Music Department
Nature of Business:
Composition festival
Design Firm:
Roman Duszek
Art Director:
Roman Duszek
Designer:
Roman Duszek

Client:
Harris Institute for the Arts
Nature of Business:
Waterfront music complex
Design Firm:
Telmet Design Associates
Art Directors:
Joseph Gault, Tiit Telmet
Designer:
Joseph Gault

Client:
Good Vibrations
Nature of Business:
Golf tournament
Design Firm:
RBMM/The Richards Group
Art Director:
Horacio Cobos
Designer:
Horacio Cobos
Illustrator:
Horacio Cobos

One of the United States' largest clothing and accessory manufacturers, VF Corporation, produces such well-known products as Wrangler and Lee jeans, Healthtex children's clothes and Jansport recreational gear. Twenty-one months into an existing five-year hardware lease, VF needed to significantly upgrade their computer equipment. In order to maintain the original lease cost on the more expensive upgraded computer equipment, VF asked to have the original lease extended. The then current lessor was unable to accommodate their needs. VF then approached El Camino and outlined their unusual requirements. El Camino worked with VF and a number of financial institutions to create a unique wrap-around lease with a lower 60-month rate and mutually agreeable terms and conditions. As the new lease now stands at the end of the original lease period, El Camino will buy the existing equipment and continue the lease or replace the equipment at no charge or rate increase to VF. VF is a prime example of El Camino's financial flexibility and complete willingness to create new and innovative programs when traditional approaches simply will not meet an individual client's requirements.

EDWARD A. THOMAS

VF CORPORATION

financing

"**EL CAMINO** gave us the lower 60-month rate on the new equipment, structured the lease just as we wanted, and (assumed all the risk). I came away **very impressed** on how hard they worked to make this deal happen." EDWARD A. THOMAS, MANAGER OF CORPORATE DP, VF CORPORATION

Client:
El Camino Resources, Inc.
Design Firm:
White Plus...
Art Director:
Trina Nuovo
Designer:
Rick Simner

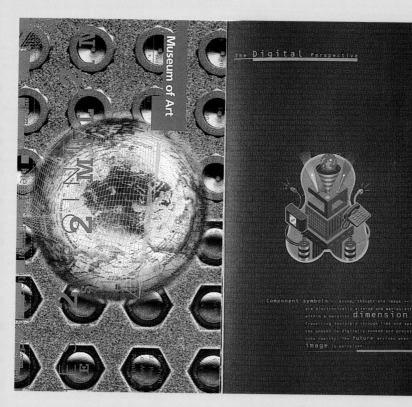

Client:
Pasifika Premier
Design Firm:
Pasifika Premier
Art Director:
Regina Rubino
Designers:
Robert Louey, Regina Rubino
Illustrator:
Steve Lyons
Photographers:
David Michael Kenedy, Rick Chu, Hanawi

Client:
Turner Entertainment Company
Nature of Business:
Media company
Design Firm:
Tracy Sabin Graphic Design
Art Director:
Alison Hill
Designer:
Tracy Sabin
Illustrator:
Tracy Sabin

Client:
Golden Harvest Films
Nature of Business:
Motion-picture distributor
Design Firm:
PPA Design
Art Director:
Byron Jacobs
Designer:
Byron Jacobs

Client:
Mike King
Nature of Business:
Photographer
Design Firm:
Sibley/Peteet Design, Inc.
Art Director:
Tom Kirsch
Designer:
Tom Kirsch
Illustrator:
Tom Kirsch

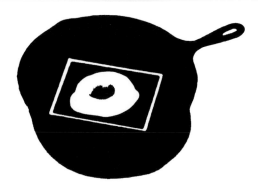

Client:
J. W. Fry
Nature of Business:
Photographer
Design Firm:
Pinkhaus
Art Director:
John Norman
Designer:
John Norman
Photographer:
John Norman

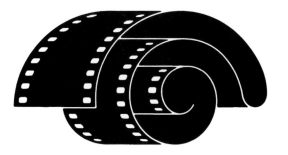

Client:
Nike, Inc.
Nature of Business:
In-house image bank
Design Firm:
Pinkhaus
Art Director:
John Norman
Designer:
John Norman
Illustrator:
John Norman

E PLURIBUS UNUM EUREKA
To Be or Not To Be *Liberté Egalité*
We the People **Time Is Money** π
E=mc² Survival of the Fittest
Knowledge Is Power **LUMINARY**

Client:
GTE Corporation
Nature of Business:
Telecommunications company
Design Firm:
GTE VisNet
Art Directors:
Timothy Bassford, Michael Meade
Designers:
Timothy Bassford, Frank Lionetti,
Michael Meade
Illustrator:
Thomas Bachman

Client:
GoodNet
Design Firm:
After Hours Creative
Art Director:
After Hours Creative
Designer:
After Hours Creative

Client:
Froytang As
Design Firm:
Pemberton & Whitefoord
Designer:
Adrian Whitefoord
Illustrator:
Simon Thomas

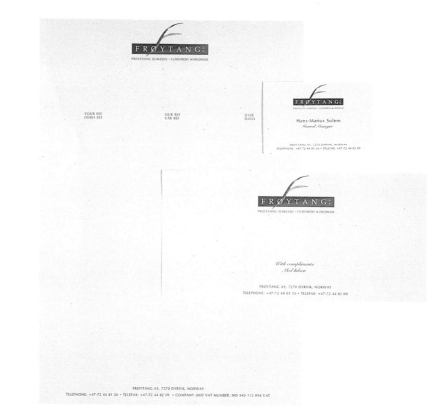

ARCHITECTURAL
DIRECTION

Client:
Sun Microsystems
Nature of Business:
Operations/architectural direction
Design Firm:
Earl Gee Design
Art Director:
Earl Gee
Designers:
Earl Gee, Fani Chung
Illustrator:
Earl Gee

Client:
3D Motion
Nature of Business:
Computer-generated animation and
architectural modeling
Design Firm:
Earl Gee Design
Art Director:
Fani Chung
Designer:
Fani Chung
Illustrator:
Fani Chung

Client:
Pacific City Land Corporation
Nature of Business:
Loft residences
Design Firm:
Siren
Art Director:
Jim Yue
Designer:
David Cheng
Illustrator:
David Cheng

Client:
California Center for the Arts
Nature of Business:
Museum
Design Firm:
Mires Design, Inc.
Art Director:
John Ball
Designers:
John Ball, Miguel Perez

Client:
The University of Ottawa
Nature of Business:
Educational institution
Design Firm:
Neville Smith Graphic Design
Art Director:
Neville Smith
Designer:
Neville Smith
Illustrator:
Neville Smith

Client:
Australian Estate Management
Nature of Business:
Commercial property management
company
Design Firm:
AGPS Design Studio
Designers:
Louise Dews, Peter Rietdyk

Client:
Atilla Öt
Nature of Business:
Fitness studio
Design Firm:
Karl Design
Art Director:
Andreas Karl
Designer:
Andreas Karl
Illustrator:
Andreas Karl

Client:
The Container Store
Nature of Business:
Home-organization store
consultation/sale
Design Firm:
Sibley/Peteet Design, Inc.
Art Director:
David Beck
Designer:
David Beck
Illustrator:
David Beck

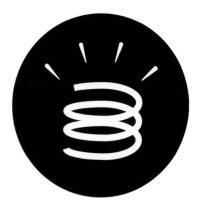

Client:
Boing! Boing! Design, Inc.
Nature of Business:
Broadcast design company
Design Firm:
Boing! Boing! Design, Inc.
Designers:
J. Roseboom, D. Williams

Client:
Moonlight Tobacco Company
Design Firm:
Cornerstone
Art Director:
Keith Steimel
Designers:
Keith Steimel, Paul McDonall
Illustrator:
Tom Montini

Client:
801 Steak & Chop House
Design Firm:
Sayles Graphic Design
Art Director:
John Sayles
Designer:
John Sayles
Illustrator:
John Sayles

Client:
Legent, XPE Software
Design Firm:
John Brady Design Consultants, Inc.
Art Directors:
Mona MacDonald, John Brady
Designers:
Kathy Kendra, Joe Tomka
Illustrator:
John Mattos

Client:
Rod Bone, Bone Dry Beer
Design Firm:
Margo Chase Design
Art Director:
Margo Chase
Designer:
Margo Chase
Photographer:
Sidney Cooper

Client:
Women's National Book
Association, Dallas (Texas) chapter
Nature of Business:
Reading group
Design Firm:
Peterson & Company
Art Director:
Nhan T. Pham
Designer:
Nhan T. Pham

Client:
Harcourt Brace & Company
Nature of Business:
Publisher, children's fantasy books
Design Firm:
Mires Design, Inc.
Art Director:
José Serrano
Designer:
José Serrano
Illustrator:
Tracy Sabin

MAGIC CARPET BOOKS

Client:
California Literacy
Nature of Business:
Literacy program
Design Firm:
Evenson Design Group
Art Director:
Stan Evenson
Designer:
Ken Loh

Client:
Washington Adventist Hospital
Foundation
Nature of Business:
Medical staff fundraising campaign
Design Firm:
Alphawave Designs
Art Director:
Douglas Dunbebin
Designer:
Douglas Dunbebin
Illustrator:
Douglas Dunbebin

Client:
Dr. Stephen Steele
Nature of Business:
Osteopathic medicine practice
Design Firm:
Bruce E. Morgan Graphic Design
Art Director:
Bruce E. Morgan
Designer:
Bruce E. Morgan

Client:
RPH On The Go USA, Inc.
Nature of Business:
Pharmaceutical temporaries
placement organization
Design Firm:
Michael Stanard, Inc.
Art Director:
Michael Stanard
Designer:
Dawn Goldammer
Illustrator:
Dawn Goldammer

Client:
Caterpillar, Inc.
Nature of Business:
Satellite TV program
Design Firm:
Simantel Group
Art Director:
Susie Ketterer
Designer:
Wendy Behrens

Truckin' Time

Client:
Tee Shirt Company
Nature of Business:
T-shirt manufacturer
Design Firm:
Mires Design, Inc.
Art Director:
José Serrano
Designer:
José Serrano

Client:
Eat More Records
Nature of Business:
Record label
Design Firm:
Lyerly Design
Art Director:
Lyerly Peniston
Designer:
Lyerly Peniston
Illustrator:
Lyerly Peniston

EAT MORE RECORDS

Client:
Spectra Interface
Design Firm:
Y's Communication
Creative Director:
Phil Young
Designer:
Simon Fuentes

Client:
XactData Corporation
Design Firm:
Hornall Anderson
Design Works, Inc.
Art Director:
Jack Anderson
Designers:
Jack Anderson, Jana Wilson,
Lisa Cerveny, Julie Keenan

Client:
Protozoa
Nature of Business:
Graphic design studio
Design Firm:
Protozoa
Art Director:
Brad deGraf
Designer:
Brad deGraf

• protozoa •

Client:
Clothes Line Inc., Joker's Eye
Nature of Business:
Clothing sub label
Design Firm:
RBMM/The Richards Group
Art Director:
Luis D. Acevedo
Designer:
Luis D. Acevedo
Illustrator:
Wayne Johnson

Client:
Lithoprep, Inc.
Nature of Business:
Pre-press organization
Design Firm:
Whaley Design
Art Director:
Kevin Whaley
Designer:
Kevin Whaley

Client:
Protozoa
Design Firm:
Protozoa
Art Director:
Brad deGraf
Designer:
Eve Lunt

Client:
Royal Hong Kong Yacht Club,
100th Anniversary
Design Firm:
PPA Design Ltd.
Art Director:
Byron Jacobs
Designer:
Byron Jacobs

Client:
ColorAd Printers
Nature of Business:
Printing company
Design Firm:
Jerry Takigawa Design
Art Director:
Jerry Takigawa
Designers:
Jay Galster, Jerry Takigawa
Illustrator:
Jay Galster

Client:
Cafe Eclipse, Fujitsu
Nature of Business:
Restaurant
Design Firm:
Swieter Design United States
Art Director:
John Swieter
Designer:
Mark Ford

Client:
Oji Paper Company, Ltd.
Nature of Business:
Paper company
Design Firm:
Packaging Create Inc.
Art Director:
Akio Okumura
Designer:
Katsuji Minami

OJI PAPER GALLERY OSAKA

VÓLO

Client:
Vólo Company, Ltd.
Design Firm:
Yoshinobu Design, Inc.
Art Director:
Takaaki Yoshinobu
Designer:
Takaaki Yoshinobu

CommSys

Client:
CommSys
Nature of Business:
Telecommunications billing service
Design Firm:
Supon Design Group
Art Directors:
Supon Phornirunlit, Andrew Dolan
Designer:
Mike LaManna

$E = MS^2$

Client:
Microsoft Corporation
Nature of Business:
Conference
Design Firm:
Hornall Anderson
Design Works, Inc.
Art Director:
Jack Anderson
Designers:
Jack Anderson, John Anicker,
David Bates

Client:
Atomic Pictures
Nature of Business:
Video/audio company
Design Firm:
Sayles Graphic Design
Art Director:
John Sayles
Designer:
John Sayles
Illustrator:
John Sayles

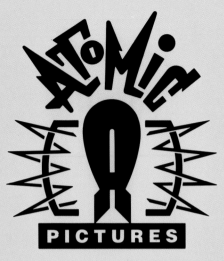

Client:
Barry Myers
Nature of Business:
Photography studio
Design Firm:
Pictogram Studio
Art Director:
Stephanie Hooton
Designer:
Hien Nguyen
Illustrator:
Hien Nguyen

Client:
American Heart Association,
Arizona Affiliate
Nature of Business:
Charity ball logo
Design Firm:
SHR Perceptual Management
Art Director:
Karin Burklein Arnold
Designer:
Nancy Ogami

ESPRIT

Client:
Loyola University Chicago,
Undergraduate Admission
Nature of Business:
Educational institution
Design Firm:
Hafeman Design Group, Inc.
Art Director:
William Hafeman
Designer:
Kurt Wisthuff

INTERACT

Client:
Moore Corporation
Nature of Business:
Information systems company,
international forum
Design Firm:
Goodooll Curtis Inc.
Art Director:
Alan MacIntyre
Designer:
Alan MacIntyre

Client:
Foote, Cone & Belding for
Adolph Coors Brewing Company
Nature of Business:
Beverage manufacturer
Design Firm:
Primo Angeli, Inc.
Art Directors:
(Primo Angeli Inc.) Primo Angeli,
Carlo Pagoda, (Libby Perszyk
Kathman) Ray Perszyk, Howard
McIlvain, (Coors) Pam Moorehead,
(FCB) George Chadwick
Designers:
(PAI) Carlo Pagoda, Ed Cristman,
Vicki Cero, (LPK) Bob Johnson,
Jim Gabel, Mary Jo Betz,
Bradd Bush, Liz Grubow,
Andy Scott, Rowland Heming

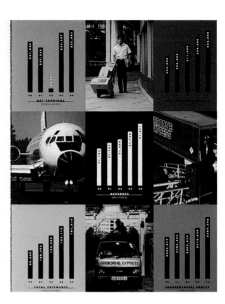

Both Advanced Logistics Services and Sky Courier are important enhancements to Airborne's core operations. They allow us to provide individualized solutions to shippers' needs and increase the range of value-added services we can offer customers.

LOOKING AHEAD TO 1995. We are cautiously optimistic about 1995, recognizing that a slower overall economy may reduce demand for domestic shipping, but hopeful that any sluggishness on the home front will be more than offset by a stronger economy in Europe and the Far East, thus helping our international operations. One of the keys to growth in the international arena, particularly for our express product, is making sure people know how to use it. Accordingly, our marketing efforts stress simplicity and ease of use in order to promote a better understanding of the product.

Our work in 1995 will include the completion of activities, begun in the fourth quarter of 1994, designed to reduce costs and improve margins on our Select Delivery Service. These will include more efficient handling of deferred deliveries through effective routing and utilization of regional hubs and daylight operations. At the same time, we will be refocusing our sales and marketing efforts to increase growth in the priority overnight service while continuing to expand sales in the deferred delivery service.

A recent development which may open up new avenues of growth, the actual specifics of which remain to be seen, is the deregulation of the intrastate trucking industry. For the most part, Airborne has not had the authority to deliver a package from one location to another within a particular state unless we took the package out of the state and brought it back in. As of January 1, 1995, regulations prohibiting Airborne's involvement in intrastate trucking activities have been abolished. We see this as a major development and one which holds great promise for expanded growth in our overnight delivery business since the more low cost shipping options there are available to customers, the more total packages will be shipped. With Airborne's efficient, low cost pick-up and delivery systems already in place, we will easily be able to accommodate the increased demand.

We are pleased to welcome Andrew F. Brimmer to our board of directors. A former Federal Reserve Board governor, he will offer valuable expertise and enhance the effectiveness of our board.

Finally, we appreciate the enthusiasm and dedication of the employees of Airborne Express, who make possible the timely delivery of needed products and services in an efficient, cost-effective manner, worldwide.

Robert S. Cline
Chairman and Chief Executive Officer

Robert G. Brazier
President and Chief Operating Officer

4

Client:
Airborne Express
Design Firm:
Hornall Anderson Design Works, Inc.
Art Director:
John Hornall
Designers:
John Hornall, Lisa Cerveny, Bruce Branson-Meyer, Heidi Favour

In the coming year, we anticipate continued high growth in sales, with contributions from the addition of more field sales Associates, more marketing agreements with partners such as PacifiCare Health Systems and the American Professional Screeners Association in the U.S., and our distribution agreement with Fotobras Fotossensiveis do Brazil Ind. Com. Ltda in Brazil.

Early in the past fiscal year we introduced two new lipid/glucose test panels, TC•HDL•Glu and Lipid Profile plus Glucose. We are pleased to report good acceptance of these panels by preventive health care professionals interested in detecting lipid disorders and diabetes. These two tests along with the recently FDA-cleared TC and Glucose test panel, give Cholestech a broader line of products to screen, at the point-of-care, for two of the most prevalent diseases affecting the world's population.

The strategic emphasis of our research and development group is to develop tests that will either expand our product line in the measurement of lipids and blood sugar or broaden our line of preventive health care screening and monitoring tests. Our R&D efforts have benefited from the fact that our technology has proven to be very flexible.

INCOR, THE BRAZILIAN HEART INSTITUTE

THE L•D•X SYSTEM WILL RECEIVE GREAT SUPPORT FROM THE BRAZILIANS BECAUSE IN THE MEDICAL POINT-OF-VIEW THIS SYSTEM HAS PROVEN TO BE ACCURATE, PRECISE AND RELIABLE AND IT PERMITS THE DOCTORS TO RECEIVE INFORMATION ABOUT LIPID PROFILE DURING THE FIRST CONSULTATION. LIPIDS ARE AN IMPORTANT RISK FACTOR FOR CORONARY HEART DISEASE, THE MOST PREVALENT CAUSE OF DEATH IN BRAZIL.

Dr. Jacqueline Scholz, M.D., Cardiologist

r e l i a b l e

Client:
Cholestech
Design Firm:
Michael Patrick Partners
Art Director:
Dan O'Brien
Designer:
Laura Dearborn
Photographer:
Mary Merrick

I N V E S T

A u s t r a l i a

Client:
The Development
Allowance Authority
Nature of Business:
Government agency
Design Firm:
AGPS Design Studio
Designer:
Keith Philip

Client:
Jeff Maul
Nature of Business:
Hair stylist
Design Firm:
Jeff Fisher Design
Art Director:
Jeff Fisher
Designer:
Jeff Fisher
Illustrator:
Jeff Fisher

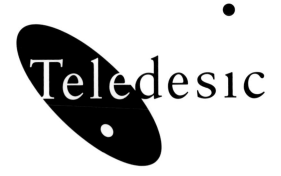

Client:
Teledesic Corporation
Nature of Business:
Wireless, satellite information
system
Design Firm:
Hornall Anderson
Design Works, Inc.
Art Director:
Jack Anderson
Designers:
Jack Anderson, Leo Raymundo

Client:
Lunar Lounge
Nature of Business:
Nightclub
Design Firm:
Swieter Design United States
Art Director:
John Swieter
Designers:
John Swieter, Jim Vogel

Client:
Barabu
Nature of Business:
Sportswear company
Design Firm:
Sayles Graphic Design
Art Director:
John Sayles
Designer:
John Sayles
Illustrator:
John Sayles

Client:
Smart Art
Nature of Business:
Home furnishings and
accessories line
Design Firm:
Sayles Graphic Design
Art Director:
John Sayles
Designer:
John Sayles
Illustrator:
John Sayles

Client:
Delmarva Power
Nature of Business:
Energy company, overhead power lines awareness campaign
Design Firm:
Delmarva Power Corporate Communications
Art Director:
John Alfred
Designer:
John Alfred
Illustrator:
John Alfred

Client:
All-Shred, Inc.
Nature of Business:
Mobile, on-site confidential document destruction
Design Firm:
Brainstorm Design
Designer:
Bob Downs

Client:
Matthews Media Group, Inc.
Nature of Business:
Young-adult health clinic
Design Firm:
Alphawave Designs
Art Director:
Douglas Dunbebin
Designer:
Douglas Dunbebin
Illustrator:
Douglas Dunbebin

Client:
Adams Golf
Nature of Business:
Golf club manufacturer
Design Firm:
Lambert Design Studio
Art Director:
Christie Lambert
Designer:
Joy Cathey Price

AIR ASSAULT

Client:
GlobalGate
Nature of Business:
Investment firm
Design Firm:
HC Design
Art Directors:
Howard Clare, Chuck Sundin

GLOBALGATE

Client:
Object F/X
Nature of Business:
Computer software company
Design Firm:
Larsen Design Office, Inc.
Art Director:
Tim Larsen
Designer:
Jerry Stenback

OBJECT|FX

Client:
Kleiner & Bold
Design Firm:
Kleiner & Bold
Designers:
Tammo F. Bruns, Frank Schulte,
Karsten Unterberger

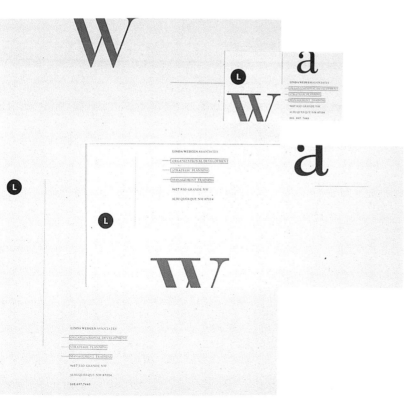

Client:
Linda Wedeen Associates
Design Firm:
Vaughn Wedeen Creative
Art Director:
Steve Wedeen
Designer:
Steve Wedeen

Client:
Croatian Tourist Association
Nature of Business:
Tourism agency
Design Firm:
Studio International
Art Director:
Boris Ljubičić
Designer:
Boris Ljubičić
Illustrator:
Boris Ljubičić
Photographer:
Damir Fabijanić

Client:
Duke City Marathon
Nature of Business:
Annual race
Design Firm:
Vaughn Wedeen Creative
Art Director:
Rick Vaughn
Designer:
Rick Vaughn
Illustrator:
Rick Vaughn

BIOPSYS

Client:
Byopsis Medical, Inc.
Nature of Business:
Makers of a rotating
breast biopsy device
Design Firm:
Andersen Jones Partners
Art Director:
Scott Marsh
Designer:
Scott Marsh

EXPERSOFT

Client:
Expersoft Corporation
Nature of Business:
Software developer
Design Firm:
Abrams Design Group
Art Director:
Colleen Abrams
Designer:
Kim Ferrell
Illustrator:
Kim Ferrell

HARVEST

Client:
Harvest Food Cooperative
Nature of Business:
Nonprofit food coop
Design Firm:
GTE VisNet
Designer:
Michael Meade

Client:
The Center for Clinical
Quality Evaluation
Nature of Business:
Healthcare research and
analysis organization
Design Firm:
Pictogram Studio
Art Director:
Stephanie Hooton
Designer:
Hien Nguyen
Illustrator:
Hien Nguyen

Client:
University of Texas, Austin
Nature of Business:
Graduate school of business
Design Firm:
Sibley/Peteet Design, Inc.
Art Director:
Rex Peteet
Designer:
Derek Welch
Illustrator:
Derek Welch

Client:
Packaging Machinery
Manufacturers Institute
Nature of Business:
On-line service
Design Firm:
William J. Kircher & Associates, Inc.
Art Director:
Bruce E. Morgan
Designer:
Bruce E. Morgan

PLANET 1 ^{SM}

Client:
ComSat
Nature of Business:
Portable phone company
Design Firm:
HC Design
Art Directors:
Howard Clare, Chuck Sundin

Qinfo INC

Client:
Qinfo Inc.
Nature of Business:
Software developer
Design Firm:
Mario Godbout Design
Art Director:
Mario Godbout
Designer:
Mario Godbout

Sc[i]³

Client:
Sunnyvale Center for Innovation,
Invention, and Ideas
Nature of Business:
Product developer
Design Firm:
Abrams Design Group
Art Director:
Colleen Abrams
Designer:
Mike Kraine
Illustrator:
Mike Kraine

Client:
Stat House
Design Firm:
Mike Salisbury Communications
Art Director:
Mike Salisbury
Designers:
Sander van Baalen, Sander Egging

KULTURSOMMER
RHEINLAND-PFALZ

Client:
Ministerium für Bildung und Kultur
Nature of Business:
Cultural event
Design Firm:
Karl Design
Art Director:
Andreas Karl
Designer:
Andreas Karl
Illustrator:
Andreas Karl

Client:
Planet Comics
Nature of Business:
Comic book store
Design Firm:
Kiku Obata & Company
Art Director:
Rich Nelson
Designer:
Rich Nelson

Client:
Weyerhaeuser
Nature of Business:
Paper company
Design Firm:
Sibley/Peteet Design, Inc.
Art Director:
Don Sibley
Designers:
Don Sibley, Tom Hough
Illustrator:
Tom Hough

Client:
Kyodo Osaka Inc.
Nature of Business:
Earth, Wind & Fire, Japan tour
Design Firm:
Kirima Design Office
Art Director:
Harumi Kirima
Designers:
Harumi Kirima, Fumitaka Yukawa

Client:
Senjakuame-Honpo Co. Ltd.
Nature of Business:
Line of candy
Design Firm:
Kirima Design Office
Art Director:
Harumi Kirima
Designer:
Harumi Kirima

Client:
Senjakuame-Honpo Co. Ltd.
Nature of Business:
Line of candy
Design Firm:
Kirima Design Office
Art Director:
Harumi Kirima
Designer:
Harumi Kirima

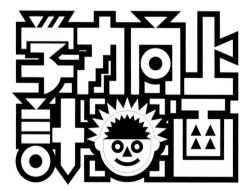

TETRA

Client:
TETRA
Nature of Business:
Manufacturer of concrete seawalls
Design Firm:
The Design Associates
Company, Ltd.
Art Director:
Tadatoshi Sato
Designers:
The Design Associates

Client:
Australian Defence Industry
Nature of Business:
Quality and Achievement Awards
Design Firm:
AGPS Design Studio
Designer:
Catriona Niven

ART IN THE GARDEN
FOUNTAIN SQUARE ARTS FESTIVAL

Client:
Evanston (Illinois) Chamber
of Commerce
Nature of Business:
Fine arts festival
Design Firm:
Michael Stanard, Inc.
Art Director:
Michael Stanard
Designer:
Kristy Vandekerckhove
Illustrator:
Kristy Vandekerckhove

Client:
Non-no Company, Ltd.
Design Firm:
DooKim Design
Art Director:
Doo H. Kim
Designers:
Dongil Lee, Seung Hee Lee

VIRTUAL
MUSIC

Client:
Ahead, Inc.
Nature of Business:
Interactive video game developer
Design Firm:
Clifford Selbert Design
Collaborative
Art Director:
Robin Perkins
Designer:
Jeff Breidenbach

Client:
Reebok
Nature of Business:
Athletic wear
Design Firm:
Heye + Partner GmbH
Art Director:
Ralph Taubenberger
Designer:
Ralf Ludwig

Client:
California Center for the Arts,
Escondido
Nature of Business:
Regional arts center
Design Firm:
Mires Design, Inc.
Art Director:
John Ball
Designers:
John Ball, Miguel Perez

Client:
Landesgartenschau Würzburg
Nature of Business:
Environmental observatory
Design Firm:
Karl Design
Art Director:
Andreas Karl
Designer:
Andreas Karl
Illustrator:
Andreas Karl

Client:
Pomurski Sejem
Nature of Business:
Agricultural and food fair
Design Firm:
KROG
Art Director:
Edi Berk
Designer:
Edi Berk

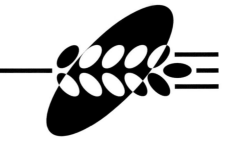

Client:
Canadian Association for
HIV Research
Nature of Business:
HIV/AIDS research organization
Design Firm:
Signals Design Group
Art Director:
Kosta (Gus) Tsetsekas
Designers:
Kosta (Gus) Tsetsekas,
Nando DeGirolamo
Illustrator:
Nando DeGirolamo

Client:
KPMG
Design Firm:
Clifford Selbert Design
Collaborative
Art Director:
Rick Simner
Designer:
Heather Watson
Illustrator:
Digital Art

LEADERSHIP

IN A CHANGING

COMPUTING

ENVIRONMENT

1994 ANNUAL REPORT

Client:
Boole & Babbage
Design Firm:
Michael Patrick Partners
Art Directors:
Dan O'Brien, Duane Maidens
Designer:
Allen Ashton
Photographers:
Sean Sullivan, Mary Merrick

Client:
Harnett's
Design Firm:
Clifford Selbert Design
Collaborative
Art Director:
Melanie Lowe
Designer:
Melanie Lowe
Photographer:
Greg Wostrel

Client:
South Pacific Special Events
Design Firm:
Value Added Design
Designer:
Heather Towns

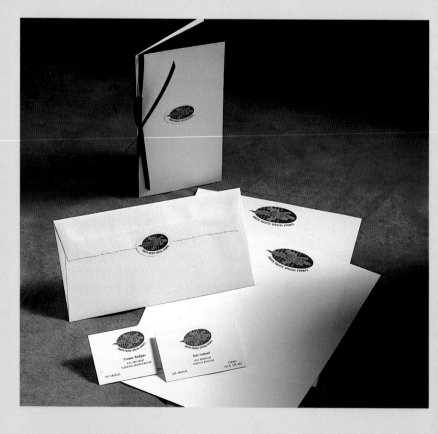

Client:
Apple Computer, Inc.,
Environmental Health
and Safety Program
Nature of Business:
Internal campaign
Design Firm:
Sheppard Associates
Art Director:
Robin Seaman
Designer:
Robin Seaman

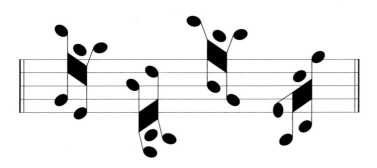

Client:
The Family Place
Nature of Business:
Children's music festival
Design Firm:
Lambert Design Studio
Art Director:
Christie Lambert
Designer:
Joy Cathey Price

Client:
Woodland Village
Nature of Business:
Retirement community
Design Firm:
DogStar Design
Designer:
Rodney Davidson
Illustrator:
Rodney Davidson

Client:
2day's Gallery
Nature of Business:
Pottery exhibit
Design Firm:
Kirby Stephens Design, Inc.
Art Director:
Kirby Stephens
Designers:
Kirby Stephens, Bill Jones
Illustrator:
Bill Jones

Client:
Birmingham (Alabama) Ecoplex
Nature of Business:
Wild animal park
Design Firm:
DogStar Design
Art Directors:
Charles Black, Stefanie Becker
Designer:
Rodney Davidson
Illustrator:
Rodney Davidson

Client:
Baptist Medical Centers
Nature of Business:
Walk-in clinic
Design Firm:
DogStar Design
Art Director:
Spencer Till
Designer:
Rodney Davidson
Illustrator:
Rodney Davidson

Client:
Trisan Home Products
Design Firm:
Brandesign
Art Director:
Barbara Harrington
Designer:
Barbara Harrington

Client:
Liberté Inc.
Design Firm:
Tarzan Communications Inc.
Art Directors:
George Fok, Daniel Fortin
Designer:
George Fok

Client:
McDonald's
Design Firm:
Heye + Partner GmbH
Art Director:
Alexander Bartel
Designer:
Oliver Diehr
Illustrator:
Oliver Diehr

Client:
Bonjour Bagel Cafe, Inc.
Design Firm:
McNulty & Company
Art Director:
Jennifer McNulty
Designer:
Jennifer McNulty
Illustrator:
Louis Chavez

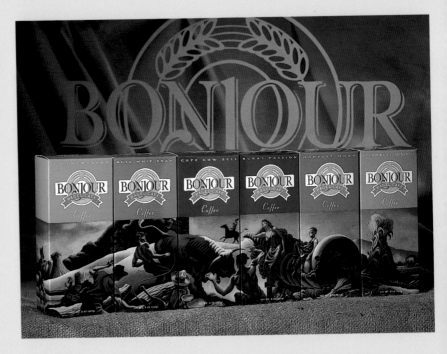

Client:
Argo Systems
Nature of Business:
Software product for
real estate appraisal
Design Firm:
RBMM/The Richards Group
Art Director:
Brian Boyd
Designers:
Brian Boyd, Horacio Cobos

Client:
Deleo Clay Tile Company
Nature of Business:
Hawaiian roofing tile maker
Design Firm:
Mires Design, Inc.
Art Director:
José Serrano
Designer:
José Serrano
Illustrator:
Tracy Sabin

Client:
Council for Exceptional Children
Nature of Business:
San Antonio (Texas) conference
Design Firm:
Johnson Design Group
Art Director:
Norasack Pathammavong
Designer:
Norasack Pathammavong

Client:
Celebrity Cruises
Nature of Business:
Leisure travel company
Design Firm:
SHR Perceptual Management
Art Director:
Miles Abernethy
Designer:
Miles Abernethy
Photographer:
Color Box, FPG International

Client:
NEON
Nature of Business:
Nonprofit Exchange
On-line Network
Design Firm:
Sam Smidt, Inc.
Art Director:
Sam Smidt
Designer:
Archie Ong

Client:
Compression Labs, Inc.
Nature of Business:
Research company
Design Firm:
SHR Perceptual Management
Art Director:
Miles Abernethy
Designer:
Miles Abernethy

Client:
Okinawa Aquarium
Design Firm:
Matsumoto Incorporated
Art Director:
Takaaki Matsumoto
Designer:
Takaaki Matsumoto

Client:
Bank of China
Design Firm:
Kan Tai-keung Design
& Associates Ltd.
Art Directors:
Kan Tai-keung, Freeman Lau Siu
Hong, Eddy Yu Chi Kong
Designers:
Kan Tai-keung, Freeman Lau Siu
Hong, Eddy Yu Chi Kong, Joyce Ho
Ngai Sing, Janny Lee Yin Wa

Client:
Washington Adventist Hospital
Foundation
Nature of Business:
Fundraising campaign
Design Firm:
Alphawave Designs
Art Director:
Douglas Dunbebin
Designer:
Douglas Dunbebin
Illustrator:
Douglas Dunbebin

Client:
Safe Space
Nature of Business:
Residential facility for
women in crisis
Design Firm:
Windsor Street Design
Associates, Inc.
Art Director:
Joan Hantz
Designer:
Joan Hantz

Client:
McGinley Associates
Nature of Business:
Odor research laboratory
Design Firm:
Design Center
Art Director:
John Reger
Designer:
Sherwin Schwartz Rock

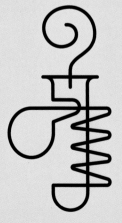

smashing plates

Client:
Jacqueline Dedell, Smashing Plates
Nature of Business:
Handpainted dining
accessories company
Design Firm:
Sibley/Peteet Design, Inc.
Art Director:
David Beck
Designer:
David Beck
Illustrator:
David Beck

Client:
Jimmie Hale Mission
Nature of Business:
Homeless shelter
Design Firm:
DogStar Design
Art Director:
Ralph Watson
Designer:
Rodney Davidson
Illustrator:
Rodney Davidson

BOROONDARA
City of Harmony

Client:
City of Booroondara (Australia)
Nature of Business:
Civil government
Design Firm:
FHA Image Design
Art Director:
Trevor Flett
Designer:
Tanja Brgoc

INDEX BY CLIENT

INDEX BY CLIENT

INDEX BY CLIENT

INDEX BY DESIGN FIRM